THE MEANING OF THE CROSS

THE MEANING
OF THE CROSS

BY

H. E. W. TURNER, D.D.

*Van Mildert Professor of Divinity in the University of Durham
and Canon Residentiary of Durham Cathedral*

LONDON

A. R. MOWBRAY & Co. LIMITED

NEW YORK: MOREHOUSE-GORHAM CO.

© *A. R. Mowbray & Co. Limited, 1959*

First published in 1959

PRINTED IN GREAT BRITAIN BY
A. R. MOWBRAY & CO. LIMITED IN THE CITY OF OXFORD
8526

TO
MY SON
CHRISTOPHER

PREFACE

THIS little book had its origin in the kind invitation of the Principal of Cuddesdon to deliver the Holy Week lectures at the College in 1958. Some years ago Messrs. A. R. Mowbray were good enough to publish a similar set of lectures delivered at Lincoln Theological College concerned with the background of the doctrine of the Atonement in the early centuries under the title of *The Patristic Doctrine of Redemption*, and this seemed an excellent opportunity to continue my study of the doctrine into more recent times. I should like here to renew my thanks to the Principal for his great kindness to a visiting lecturer and to the help given by both staff and students in individual and group-discussion to clarify the argument where it was needlessly obscure.

Some of the material was used as the basis for the Lenten Addresses in Durham Cathedral during the same year, and I am most grateful to the Dean and to my colleagues of the Cathedral Chapter for allowing me to share with them and with members of the Cathedral congregation my efforts to renew my understanding of the meaning of the Cross.

In my undergraduate days I remember hearing H. R. Mackintosh lecturing on the subject at a Student Christian Movement Conference at Swanwick. I have long since forgotten practically everything that he said, but one observation has remained in my mind: 'We think that we do not understand the Cross because we are not clever enough. There is a deeper reason yet. It is because we are not good enough.' The truth of this statement has been borne in on me increasingly over the years, and never so much as during the preparation and delivery of these lectures. For in our thinking about the Cross we are not concerned with pushing around a set of intellectual counters until they fit into the kind of pattern which pleases us. We are concerned with something which stands close to the roots of our being. If we were better people, more 'personal' people, we should come nearer to the heart of the matter. Anyhow, let us make the attempt to understand together and see how we get on.

H. E. W. TURNER

CONTENTS

9

The Meaning of the Cross

CHAPTER I

SETTING THE STAGE

It is one of the tests of the truth of Christianity that every Christian doctrine keys into every other doctrine, so that it is impossible to discuss any single doctrine without being involved sooner or later in the whole range of Christian theology.[1] This is particularly the case with the doctrine of the Atonement. The charge of implying an inadequate doctrine of God (if it is substantiated) is a decisive argument against any particular theory. It almost goes without saying that Christology is deeply involved, for the Atonement is directly related to the death of Christ. But is it primarily an act wrought by Christ as God or as Man, or is it, in fact, two-sided? How is the Atonement related to the whole process of the Incarnate Life, Death, and Resurrection? Again, what is the human predicament to which the Atonement is addressed? What is man, and what is the nature of the sin from which the Cross delivers him? Is sin fundamentally a privative or a negative, an absence of knowledge, a misdirection of will, or a defect of nature? How is the Atonement mediated through the life of the Church, and how is it

[1] See, for example, K. E. Kirk, *The Coherence of Christian Doctrine.*

11

applied to the life of the individual or to the world at large? It is easier to frame such questions than to answer them, and clearly in a short treatment of so great a theme much must be omitted or handled in the briefest of fashions. And it is inevitable that, even when all is said, some will consider the answers to such questions inadequate or unsatisfactory.

There is also the cognate question of what Professor Hodgson has called the general outlook of different periods or theologians.[1] The context of a particular theologian and the human situation which he treats as the natural environment for his solution are important 'non-theological factors' in the doctrine of the Atonement. The Cross has been considered in turn against the backcloth of the law-court, the feudal system, and even the market-place, with mingled elements of truth and error. Perhaps the nearest modern counterpart is the psychiatrist's clinic.

In his fine book, *The Pattern of Atonement*, Professor Hodges speaks somewhat disparagingly of 'the atmosphere of the driest theological speculation, whose relation to the actual Christian life is apt to appear somewhat tenuous, which pervades the somewhat dreary catalogue of the theories of the past.[2] His own treatment is fresh and invigorating, always closely concerned with the actualities of the Christian life. I am, however, convinced myself that from the previous mapping of the ground there will emerge with sufficient clarity the main problems which a satisfactory doctrine of the Atonement must try to meet, together with

[1] L. Hodgson, *The Doctrine of the Atonement*, pp. 141–2.
[2] H. A. Hodges, *The Pattern of Atonement*, p. 10.

important suggestions for their treatment. There may well prove to be an intolerable deal of chaff mixed with the wheat, or an abundance of false trails which (if pursued to their conclusion) would make nonsense of the experience which they are designed to explain. If, however, we 'demythologize' the theories of the past, and try to discover the real pressures of thought which lie behind their somewhat forbidding exterior, we may find ourselves in possession of important clues for our reconsideration. It is a striking, but not altogether unexpected, fact that recent discussions of the doctrine normally find in the older theories an admixture of truth and error, a wealth of partial but unrelated insights. Among the major problems which beset a student of the doctrine of the Atonement is the need to focus these insights, and to build into a coherent structure material which has too frequently been treated in isolation.

The remainder of this chapter will be devoted to a preliminary consideration of some major questions which will become increasingly important as the argument proceeds.

1. *Is the Atonement Objective or Subjective?*

This is the classical division of theories of the Atonement which goes back to the time of St. Anselm and Abelard. In brief conclusion it would appear as if each side had made out its own case, without, however, being able to exclude the elements of truth contained in the rival view. The situation is not without parallel in other departments of theology.

Further reflexion suggests adequate reasons why

this should be the case. Reduced to their simplest form, the truths for which the two schools of thought contend may be expressed as follows. The objective view maintains that 'He did it for me,' while subjective theories assert that 'He died to make us good.' But these statements are supplementary rather than contradictory, and both are needed for any interpretation of the Atonement. Theological sympathy has oscillated between these two poles, but recent theological study is coming increasingly to recognize that any theory which claims to be adequate must do justice to both insights.

The strength of objective views lies in the recognition that the Atonement is grounded in the action of God Himself. It is not a mere device, effective with some psychological types, for making us better. God has taken and retained the initiative in action, costly and redemptive action. Yet this fact has often been presented in wrong ways or in inadequate terms. It has been interpreted as effecting a change in God Himself, which, if it were possible, could only be for the worse, or as the reconciliation of the Divine attributes of Justice and Mercy set, as it were, at loggerheads with each other. With greater justice it has been regarded as primarily an act of the Divine Mercy, which nevertheless made full provision for the moral order of the universe. But this moral order has been conceived as independent of or, as it were, external to God Himself, something set over against God which He must in some way satisfy in His quest for sinful man. The background imagery of the doctrine, the law-court, feudal society, or even the chaffering of the market-place, has not greatly strengthened the presentation of these theories. At worst these are transient images, and at best they fall below the highest ranges of human existence. In all but the noblest forms of this group of theories the divine action tends to be expressed in terms of a transaction, sometimes expressed in an external way, and always in danger of importing an element of artificiality into their interpretation. Yet, as Dr. Hodgson rightly reminds us, the sense of 'something accomplished, something done' cannot easily be removed from our understanding of the Atonement.[1] Divine action, costly, vicarious, and victorious, is of its very essence. There is an act of God which is theologically prior to the process of moral and spiritual betterment which flows from the Cross.

On the other hand, the subjective view rightly claims that no theory of the Atonement can stand which is taken in isolation from the actuality of a new life, from a redeemed existence here and now. The Cross is the source of the deepest and most permanent streams of Christian living. Grave difficulties, however, arise if this insight is not combined with other and more objective aspects of the doctrine of the Atonement. Whether the Cross is conceived primarily in terms of a supreme revelation of the Divine Love or, more narrowly, as a powerful and convincing human example, it is not easy to see how this can atone for the past as well as avail in the present. On such theories how can the Cross of Christ atone (as on any reasonable showing it surely must) for those who have never heard the Christian message? Do theories of this kind set an unfair premium upon the possession of a certain

[1] L. Hodgson, op. cit., p. 13 (cp. p. 50).

sympathetic imagination which warms to the Cross and enters readily into the meaning of the sufferings of Christ? The double aspect of the Atonement as offer and demand is intolerably reduced if human response is to be of the order of 'It appeals' or 'It does not appeal' to me. It may be doubted whether such theories really afford the answer to man's need at its deepest and most interior level.

It is significant that the two theories which seem to have most to commend them—the Ethical Satisfaction theory and the doctrine of Vicarious Suffering—combine elements taken from both schools of thought. The former lays great emphasis upon the obedience of Christ even unto death. Here is alike an action and a moral impulse. It is something yielded to God which man had proved signally and constitutionally incapable of rendering, but at the same time it evokes a response in ourselves which it proves powerful to supply. Again, vicarious suffering is at once an action on God's part, taking upon Himself in Christ something which is not only one consequence of human sin, but also a powerful motive of alienation from Himself, and the most potent means of moral and spiritual improvement in ourselves.

We should therefore be fully justified in concluding that any adequate theory of the Atonement must satisfy the double test of objectivity and subjectivity.

2. *Is the Atonement to be understood as the act of Christ as God towards man, or as the act of Christ as Man before God?*

The doctrine of Redemption has important implications in the field of Christology. As I have tried to show

elsewhere, they played a major part in the development
of the doctrine in the Patristic period.[1] In discussing
the doctrine of vicarious victory, which Bishop Aulén
describes as the classical theory, I suggested a distinction which did not seem to have received the attention
which it deserved. Some phrasings of the doctrine
virtually amounted to a *Logos Victor* theory, while
other forms equally plainly presupposed a *Christus
Victor*. The vital difference lay in whether the victory
was attributed to our Lord as God or as Man. The
two streams approximate somewhat closely to the two
classical Christologies of the period, the Monist and the
Dualist, or, as Professor Richard has characterized
them, the *Verbum caro* and the *Verbum homo* traditions.[2]
Their principal difference lay in their estimate of the
humanity of our Lord, a divergence which has obvious
repercussions for Christian spirituality, and may even
have arisen in this field. The Monist maintains that the
Logos is firmly in control of the Incarnate Person and
claims that, notwithstanding the human conditions
under which it is accomplished, redemption must be
centrally and essentially a Divine act if it is to be
universally transmitted to men. A victory won by the
Incarnate Logos is universally available; a victorious
human personality could only deliver his own soul by
his righteousness. The Dualist, on the other hand,
works with a completely different methodology. The
humanity of our Lord is not merely the human conditioning of the Logos in the Divine act of redemption;

[1] H. E. W. Turner, *The Patristic Doctrine of Redemption*, pp. 47–69.
[2] This schema of Professor M. Richard is expounded in A. Grill-
meier and H. Bacht, *Das Konzil von Chalcedon*, pp. 5–202.

B

it plays an indispensable part in the economy of salvation, and unless it were complete, the very existence of redemption would be jeopardized. A victory won essentially by the Logos could not avail for our salvation, since the struggle which it involves would be unreal. It might almost be described as an exhibition of shadow-boxing rather than as a genuine victory won at cost.

A similar, but somewhat less sharp-set divergence can be found in more recent theories. Objective views normally lay the emphasis upon what Christ has done as Man towards God. He satisfies God's outraged honour, or pays some sort of debt contracted by the fact of sin. Subjective views, however, can point either way. They can either regard the Cross as the revelation of the Love of God to man, or as a supreme moral example presented to men by Christ as Man.

Once again the logic of the situation appears to demand both. In any approach to the doctrine of the Atonement, the double solidarity of our Lord with God as well as with ourselves must be fully utilized. Perhaps it is not an unfair criticism of some theories of the Atonement that they seem to work with less than the full Chalcedonian Christology.

3. *What is the relation between the Atonement and the whole pattern of the Incarnation which includes the historical ministry and the Resurrection as well as the Cross?*

Here there seem to be two modern tendencies. It is an interesting fact that Evangelical schools of theology normally place the emphasis upon the work of Christ, whereas more Catholic approaches lay greater stress upon His Person. This is, of course, a generalization, and it is exposed to the usual dangers of such statements. Perhaps little more is at stake than the nomenclature of certain university courses! In any case, no lectures on Christology can afford to neglect the work of Christ, while any account of His work must be based upon an adequate doctrine of His Person. Yet there is a certain truth in the description by a Lutheran scholar, Professor Einar Molland, of the Evangelical Churches as Good Friday Churches; of the Orthodox Churches as Churches of Easter Day; and of the Church of England as *par excellence* the Church of Christmas Day.[1] Differences, in perspective at least, can be traced both in theology and liturgy. Those who devote most attention to the work of Christ seem at times to think of Him as *mori missus* (sent to die), as though His atoning death could be taken in isolation from His saving life. At the opposite end of the scale, such attention may be devoted to the earthly ministry of our Lord as a whole as almost to disperse the significance of the Cross, or to regard it as merely a single act within a total process.

There is, of course, an element of truth in both extremes. The former view is concerned above all to assert the cruciality of the Cross as the craggy unrepeatable upon which our salvation depends, but it may sometimes obscure the fact that ultimately it is not the Cross, but the Person Crucified in His totality

---

[1] Some implications of the description of the Eastern Orthodox Church as the Church of the Resurrection are criticized in E. L. Mascall, *The Recovery of Unity*, pp. 70–1.

who is unique and redemptive. Only one Cross on the
hill of Calvary was the answer to the world's need; the
two companion crosses merely formed part of the
problem. Here both the problem and its answer were
set side by side. The latter view rightly notes that the
whole life, teaching, and mighty works of Jesus form
part of a single redemptive pattern with His Death and
Resurrection. This fact alone serves to explain what is
inevitably a difficulty on the alternative view, the fact
that our Lord could forgive sins during His earthly life.
Yet, if the redeeming Person is already present, the
crucial act of redemption had not as yet taken place.
Without the Cross the answer to the indignant question
of the Pharisees, 'Who can forgive sins but God alone?'
would have remained incomplete. If the danger of the
first view is to see in the Cross an unrelated peak, the
second view tends to merge its significance into a kind
of 'flatland' perspective of our redemption.

It is therefore of the utmost importance in thinking
about the Atonement to seek for bridge-words which
can apply both to the Cross and to the earthly life in
which it is set without reducing the significance of
either. Among these we may well find that terms like
'obedience,' 'suffering,' and 'victory' will serve us best.
But the Cross does not merely point backwards into
the earthly ministry of our Lord; it also looks forward
to the Resurrection and beyond. To consider the Cross
is also to imply the Resurrection. For without the
Resurrection, the Cross would be Tragedy instead of
Victory. Its final message would be man's 'No' rather
than God's 'Yes.' And any full-scale treatment would
need to devote considerable attention to the work of

the Holy Spirit and the heavenly intercession of the Risen and Ascended Lord. Not all Christian traditions would, however, continue in the same way. Here I suggest that those who regard the Cross as the saving Event are inclined to give most place to the Holy Spirit as making real to the believing Christian the fruits and benefits of the Passion of our Lord, whereas those who think most naturally of the Cross as part of a whole redemptive process achieved throughout the earthly ministry tend rather to emphasize the continuation or extension of the Incarnation through the Church which is His Body. The one stream thinks most naturally of appropriation, the other of incorporation. Possibly this difference (if I have grasped its significance aright) has more to do with differences concerning the doctrine of the Church than has sometimes been thought. We shall discover later that it has a direct bearing on the doctrine of Justification, which has recently become once again a living issue within the Church of England itself.

4. *Is the Cross 'cosmic' or parochial?*

At least in this form this question has probably never occurred to most readers of this book; indeed, its very significance may be obscure. But a study of Oliver Quick's fine book, *The Gospel of the New World*, discloses a point of real substance here. We are accustomed to think of the Atonement in terms of a rescue operation directed towards the human race, and we do well. But are we in danger of missing a whole further range of meaning by restricting it too narrowly to this particular purpose? Would this be too 'parochial' a task to be fully adequate to the far-reaching significance of the Cross of Christ? In raising this question I am not forgetting the principle that 'nothing is more worthy of God than man's salvation.' The term 'parochial' is not intended to deny that human redemption is an important, even a vital, 'parish.' But redeemed man also lives in a redeemed universe, and a world in which the Cross and Resurrection of Jesus Christ have taken place can never be the same again. It is at least in this respect a radically different universe, and must be revalued in the light of these decisive and redemptive events. It will clearly be necessary to devote closer attention to this question in a later chapter.

CHAPTER II

MAN'S PREDICAMENT

BEFORE embarking upon our discussion of the doctrine of the Atonement, it is advisable, even at the risk of some repetition, to offer some diagnosis of the human situation of which the Cross is the Divine remedy.

A sixteenth-century Anglican writer, Sir Thomas Browne, a Norwich doctor, describes man as 'the Great Amphibium,' an inhabitant of two worlds, earth and heaven. This is the paradox of man which differentiates him from the rest of creation. It is his glory, but it is also part of the question mark which is set against his nature, for it exposes him to the danger of concentrating upon one part of his heritage at the expense of the other. He may become so involved in the earth, its concerns and interests, as to forget his other home-land—and that we call materialism; or he may become so engrossed in heavenly concerns and interests as to neglect the other environment in which he has been placed. This is described by St. Augustine as 'the angelic fallacy,' and gives rise to the misguided attempt to become more 'spiritual' than God intended man to be.[1] The paradoxical situation to which this double setting of human life leads might be expressed somewhat crudely as follows: 'Matter matters, but matter does not matter most.' Each of these equal and

[1] See Visser T'Hooft, *The Renewal of the Church*, p. 13.

opposite errors has its own appropriate penalty. Materialism, practical as well as theoretical, means a loss of moorings, a soul adrift, while a false and exaggerated spirituality leads to a lack of concern, an attempted disengagement from the world, with grave implications not only for the soul of the individual, but also for the life of the community in which he lives. And these two tendencies represent temptations not only for individual Christians, but also in greater or lesser degree for Christian groups and even for whole Churches at different periods of their history.

But this paradox of man's nature strikes deeper yet. Man is a creature, but possesses a kind of delegated sovereignty over the universe in which he is placed. He has the power to think God's thoughts after Him and thus to understand his world. He is able in no small measure to control his world, though, curiously enough, he finds self-mastery and life in community an even more difficult task. His freedom, however, always remains a creaturely freedom, and where this is forgotten it inevitably gets out of balance. It can lead to the attempt to forget that he is a creature, and to exalt himself at the expense of his Creator. This is clearly set out in the old Hebrew account of the origin of evil.[1] Here the root of man's sin is not the unnatural craving for forbidden fruit. The Rubicon has already been crossed when that stage is reached, when the woman yields to the temptation implicit in the serpent's question, 'Yea, hath God said?' The hard core of sin, whether in the first rudimentary stumblings of a Dawn Man or in the more complex situation of contemporary

[1] Gen. iii. 1–21.

society, is not lust, but pride, and pride leading to disobedience. The affirmation of self-will against God's purpose for his life may serve as a rough and approximate definition of human sin.

Man is therefore not merely a creature, but a fallen creature. He has, as it were, stepped out of his proper frame of reference and is faced with the fact of sin. He hears the voice of the Lord God in the garden and is afraid. He knows himself to be naked and hides himself.

Man may sin for many reasons. The cause may be human weakness when the power of the flesh or the pressure of his environment overcomes his best intentions. He may sin through muddle-headedness which leads to confusion as to the issues involved or the right choice to make. In moral conduct there is urgent need for the discipline of calling things by their right names. We often need to remind ourselves (or to be reminded by others), 'That's pride, lust, temper, or selfishness,' or the like. This may be illustrated even outside the confines of Christianity from a poem preserved in the Dead Sea Scrolls, which is described by its editor, Dr. T. H. Gaster, as the Hymn of the Initiants. In his translation the passage reads as follows:

> I shall hold it as one of the laws
> Engraven of old on the tablets,
> To face my sin and transgression
> And to avouch the justice of God.[1]

One familiar New Testament description of sin is 'missing the mark' ($\dot{\alpha}\mu\alpha\rho\tau\iota\alpha$) or 'falling short of the glory of God.' Yet sin is a good deal more than a

[1] T. H. Gaster, *The Scriptures of the Dead Sea Sect*, p. 124.

student's first attempt at an examination question which can be crossed out and started again without any further consequence than loss of time or wasted effort.

In the history of the doctrine of the Atonement special emphasis has been placed upon five aspects of sin, and it is to these that we must next devote brief attention.

1. *Sin as Transgression*

Here the concept of sin is carried a stage further. The rabbis drew a famous distinction between deliberate sin (sin with a high hand) and sins of ignorance, and the same contrast reappears in Christian moral theology in the classification of sins as 'material' and 'formal.' Sin includes an element of deliberate challenge to a known norm which is rightly characterized as transgression. It is to know where our duty lies, and yet deliberately to choose something else. It amounts to an attempt to engage in a private treaty with the moral law, an ethical 'It can't happen here.' It is as though we were to say (for example), 'Murder is, of course, wrong for most people in most circumstances; but not for me here and now.' It implies the recognition of a moral standard which is known and accepted by man as a norm, and yet which is broken by his sin.

This deliberate challenge has a twofold framework of reference. For the moral law is no arbitrary restriction upon human freedom; it is, in effect, the precondition of real liberty. When man sins, he violates the very principles of his own existence. He is virtually 'cutting off his nose to spite his face.' But since this law is the ethical norm which God has laid down for His creatures, the challenge involved in transgression is directed not merely against man's own proper being, but also against the sovereignty of God who is Himself its Author and Guarantor.

2. *Sin as Disobedience*

The description of sin as transgression almost inevitably suggests something cold, impersonal, and even external, like the infringement of a by-law or the breach of a regulation. But sin goes even deeper than that. It is the rebellion of a creature against its Creator, the disobedience of a subject against his king. It is, therefore, an offence against a Person with rights over us, the usurpation of a liberty which does not belong to us. In purely human relations our view of the seriousness of misdemeanours varies directly with the extent to which the interests of other people are directly involved. Thus a parking offence looms less largely in our eyes than an offence against a person. Sin contains a similar personal reference, for it is an act of disobedience committed against our Creator, who has set the moral law as the compass for our lives as well as an act of rebellion against One to whom we owe our obedience as of right. Seen against the context of feudal society with its carefully graded series of rights and duties, this is how St. Anselm interpreted the nature of sin. The same idea set against the backcloth of absolute monarchy recurs in the thought of a later age. It still retains its due measure of truth, even in the context of our own egalitarian society.

3. *Sin as Estrangement*

The same fundamental idea of sin as an offence against a person is carried immeasurably deeper when it is seen in the light of the deeper relationships of human life, such as of friend to friend, husband to wife, and parent to child. No relationship of this kind can be free and uninhibited if it is hindered by conduct liable to cause estrangement. The initial causes of such estrangement may not appear serious in themselves. A broken marriage may start with something comparatively trivial which nevertheless proves to be the rift within the lute. A breach of this kind always tends to widen alarmingly unless action is taken to close the gap. Unhealed relationships are never restored automatically by the mere passage of time. Here the initiative is most appropriately taken by the one who has suffered the wrong, and the way to reconciliation always lies along the path of suffering love.

It has been well said that sin is anything which blocks us from God or from other people. Unrepented and unforgiven sin sets up a barrier between God and man, and the breach which it causes inevitably widens as time goes on. The first effect of sin, here as elsewhere, is to be fruitful and multiply both in the life of an individual and in the corporate experience of the human race. In consequence, it has become an indisputable fact that man no longer finds himself at home with God. Man the prodigal experiences fear, guilt, and spiritual deadness in the Divine Presence, in place of his true inheritance of freedom, joy, and peace.

4. *Sin as Frustration*

Sir Oliver Lodge once asserted that 'modern man is no longer worried about his sins.' Victorian optimism has, however, yielded place, even in many humanistic circles, to a more sober mood, and the psychiatrist's clinic affords contemporary evidence that the sins of modern man have certainly not ceased to 'worry' him. A healthy and integrated personality cannot be built round a behaviour-pattern of this kind.

Attention has already been directed to the importance of calling things by the right names, and of dealing with them on their proper level. Unrepented and unforgiven sin eats like an acid into the personality, and sinks below the level of consciousness with incalculable results. The turbulence of youth with its angry and ostentatious rebellion against things in general, as well as some of the more outwardly respectable phenomena of middle age, with its narrowing of compass and retraction of interest, appear to spring from this cause. Frustration and sin march together and in extreme cases even threaten the very integrity of the self as a unitary being. Perhaps, in relatively mild forms, schizophrenia is more common than is often thought. It is perhaps significant that the psychologist no less than the theologian uses the concept of guilt, though he often sets it against a wholly different background.

5. *Sin as Disorder*

Finally, sin may be described as disorder, as living against the grain of the spiritual universe. In a period in which 'Do it yourself' has become a popular slogan, it is a familiar fact that there are two ways of sawing wood, with or against the grain. There is a texture in wood with which it is important to co-operate in any attempt to control it. In a far deeper sense this is true of life itself. The moral law is not only normative for human behaviour; it is a leading principle in our interpretation of the universe itself. Because life comes from God and tends to God, it possesses a certain texture which we ignore at our peril. Sin considered as disorder can therefore be regarded as a bad case of living 'against the grain' of the spiritual world.

Man's predicament is not merely a case of particular acts of sin. He not only commits what a theologian would call 'actual sins'; he is also involved in original sin. While there are many theories of the nature and cause of original sin which should be treated with some reserve, the fact which underlies them seems quite undeniable. There is a race history of alienation from God which makes wrong acts of choice fatally easy. Sin multiplies in the history of the human race no less than in the life of the individual. Our heredity as well as our environment is tainted by sin. A sinful character is not simply built up from a succession of wrong choices; they appear to spring from a sinful character. The fruit springs from a root, and it is deep within man's nature that the trouble really lies.

Such, then, is man's predicament, the situation to which God has provided the answer in Christ. St. Paul had a word for it. In the Epistle to the Romans he describes Israel as 'hostile, yet beloved.'[1] And here (apart from the Cross) stands not only Israel, but the whole human race.

[1] Rom. xi. 28.

CHAPTER III

THE GUIDING CLUES: THE JURIDICAL

OUR next task is to survey five types of theory of the Atonement, each following a major clue to the understanding of the Cross and set against a different context or background of thought, and to suggest the elements of permanent value which they contain. The accepted principles of the feudal system which formed the background of the thought of St. Anselm have long since passed from the stage of actuality, but the machinery of the law-courts is still with us, and we shall need to inquire whether it suggests any elements of permanent truth which still need to be incorporated into any account of the Atonement. Some dominant trends in recent thinking about the Cross have their roots in the personalist philosophy of the early years of the present century. Psychological medicine has certain important suggestions to offer. Up to the present, however, the contemporary Welfare State and, still more, the technological age which is widely heralded at the moment, have not proved exactly fertile in ideas and images which are readily capable of reinterpretation in a theological idiom. While these guiding clues might seem to belong more appropriately to a sociological history of theology, they may still retain a certain significance in a study of the doctrine of the Atonement which is not exhausted by the social and intellectual milieu in which they were first applied.

31

The juridical approach to the doctrine of the Atonement interprets man's predicament mainly in terms of transgression, a deliberate passing of permitted bounds or the breach of a known norm. Such theories usually regard this norm not only as the law of man's own being, an ideal which is regulative for human relationships, but also as constituting part of the fabric of the universe itself. Attention has often been drawn to two striking facts about the moral law. We are familiar enough with hypothetical or restricted imperatives of the type, 'If you wish to get a good degree, you ought to work hard.' These, however, fall below the level of moral obligation, though their objectives may well form part of a moral purpose. If the goal is changed, the imperative no longer applies. On the other hand, the moral law comes to us with the force of an absolute and unconditional imperative. The relativity of the content of our moral judgements is not a valid objection here, since the harder it is pressed, the more difficult it becomes to account for the absolute form of the obligation which they carry with them. A similar situation exists with truth and probably also with beauty. In each case it is more natural to speak of a relative and imperfect apprehension of an absolute standard than to disperse part of the evidence by 'relativizing' the norm itself.

There is a further curious fact about our moral experience which seems to carry us more deeply still into the roots of our being. We can only have an obligation to act in a certain way, but we only assign the highest ethical value to right actions done from a good motive. Against such, as St. Paul might have said, there is no law. I have an obligation to pay my taxes; indeed, the State will step in and see that I do so. But the highest ethical worth is only assigned to the payment of taxes willingly and cheerfully. Here, then, ethics seems to pass beyond itself into regions for which it cannot fully provide.[1] Man has normally taken the existence of the moral law into account as one of his main clues to the interpretation of the universe. Once this law is seen to have its source and ground in the character of God Himself it becomes natural to describe it as not merely regulative of human conduct in particular, but constitutive at its own level of the universe itself.

The conception of sin as transgression is closely related to the Biblical doctrine of God as Judge. This is presented in the Gospel tradition in two complementary ways. In their present form, the Synoptic Gospels emphasize the Judgement at the Parousia, while the Fourth Evangelist prefers to focus his attention upon the judgement of Christ as the standing condition of His Incarnate Life. Yet neither component part of the tradition ignores completely the characteristic features of the other. Whether or not Professors Dodd and Jeremias are justified in seeking to detach the Synoptic Parables of Judgement from their present theological setting in the Gospels (*Sitz im Leben*), it is at least clear that the Judgement of our Lord at His coming in glory will be but the final consummation of a process which

---

[1] For the distinction between the categorical and the hypothetical imperatives see Kant, *The Metaphysic of Morals*. Sir David Ross in his book, *The Right and the Good*, calls attention to the other distinction noted in the passage.

C

has already begun.[1] Jewish institutions, social conventions, and methods of thought are already being judged in the Gospels by our Lord's attitude towards them. Individuals and religious groups are under judgement in their attitude to Him. In the trials before Caiaphas, Herod, and Pilate, judge and prisoner in effect change places. And this process of judgement, already begun in the household of God, will continue until the end of time.

Judgement involves punishment. Here Dr. Hodgson offers a careful defence of the notion of punishment as retributive, and even as vindictive in the proper sense of the words.[2] Judgement is retributive in relation to the past; it is retrospective in character. It can also be described as vindictive in the restricted sense that it vindicates a norm against a challenge. Indeed, it might be argued that this view of punishment alone can satisfy the definition of a person as a being with rights and duties. It insists upon a twofold truth. On the one hand, it asserts that punishment can never be made an excuse for 'messing about' with an individual life, the liquidation of a social misfit or the brain-washing of an ideological heretic, while, on the other hand, it also secures to the community the right to deal with a serious challenge to its accepted norms. The human

[1] See C. H. Dodd, *Parables of the Kingdom*, and J. Jeremias, *The Parables of Jesus*. In a recent study, *Jesus and His Coming*, Dr. J. A. T. Robinson urges that the association of the Last Judgement with the Parousia, though undoubtedly contained in the Gospels as we have them, does not belong to the teaching of Jesus Himself. Though his thesis is brilliantly argued and persuasively urged, it seems to me at least to fall some considerable distance short of being conclusive.

[2] L. Hodgson, op. cit., pp. 52–67.

judge to whom the community entrusts its own vindica-
tion against the offender is (in this context) impersonal.
He must be detached from any personal involvement
in the situation with which he is commissioned to deal.
He may thus be called upon to administer a law with
which he personally disagrees.

When we describe God's disapproval of sin in terms
of judgement, care must clearly be taken over the
method of presentation. The phrase, 'the wrath of
God,' or, more widely, 'the wrath,' is certainly Biblical,
but it can be subject to the most grotesque misunderstanding.[1] It must not be separated from another New
Testament expression, 'the wrath of the Lamb.' It
cannot therefore be interpreted as the anger, still less
as the petulance, of God. A more common error is to
regard it as an attribute utterly alien or diametrically
opposed to His Love. Perhaps we shall approximate
most nearly to the truth in describing it as the cutting-
edge of His Love. It is the same God who judges and
saves, and, although we may well hesitate to identify
these two operations, they clearly have an integral
connexion with each other.[2] God is neither merely the
inflexible Judge, nor simply the compassionate Father.
The God who shows His 'almighty power most chiefly
in showing mercy and pity' is also the ultimate home

---

[1] 'The wrath of God,' Jn. iii. 36, Rom. i. 18, Col. iii. 6; 'The wrath
to come,' Mt. iii. 7, Lk. iii. 7 (Q), 1 Thess. i. 10; 'The wrath,' Rom. ii.
5, 8, iv. 15, v. 9, ix. 22, Eph. ii. 3, v. 6, 1 Thess. ii. 16, v. 9; 'The wrath
of the Lamb,' Rev. vi. 16; His wrath, Rev. vi. 17, xi. 18, xvi. 19. A
recent study of the whole theme may be found in A. T. Hanson's
book, *The Wrath of the Lamb*.

[2] See J. Langton Clarke, *The Eternal Saviour Judge*, for a full exploration of this theme.

and source of the moral order of the universe. Even here, however, caution is required; for this moral order is neither an entity outside God to which He must conform, nor yet a factor which His forgiveness can neglect to maintain. His relationship to the moral order is not, as it were, extrinsic, but intrinsic. It is not a necessity imposed upon Him from without, but His own sign-manual in the universe which He has created. It is a fact which must not merely be safeguarded, but taken (if possible) into the whole process of redemption. Further, in contrast to the human judge, God is in the fullest possible sense involved or engaged in the situation with which He is confronted.

This clue to the understanding of the Atonement also corresponds to man's consciousness of his own predicament. Recognizing that sin is transgression and facing God as His Judge, man cannot evade the vital question, 'How can I, a lost and guilty sinner, come before a just and holy God?' Man needs a new status before God and finds it through the merits of the Atoning Death of Christ.

On this view the Cross of Christ is considered primarily as an instrument, an action performed by Christ as Man before God. In no merely formal sense Christ is our substitute and sin-bearer. God has laid on Him the iniquities of us all. He is on the Cross because by rights we should be there ourselves. It has even been customary for such theories to speak of a transference of punishment from us to Him, though protests have often been raised against the whole idea as fundamentally immoral. These objections might well be sustained if the transference were regarded as an accidental or wholly external transaction. Perhaps, however, the problem may be clarified by two human analogies, from which an important distinction may emerge. A wealthy stranger pays the fine of a prisoner with whom he has had no previous connexion, and then drives off from the court without taking any further interest in the man whose release he has thus secured. The prisoner would certainly go free under the conditions of human justice, but we should describe the action of his benefactor as quixotic rather than redemptive just because of the complete absence of any personal relationship either before or after his action. On the other hand, within the family circle a father might bear the simple punishment imposed by a mother upon their child. His action might well bring home, as nothing else could, the injury suffered by the family as a whole through the child's misdemeanour. Its redemptive significance is directly related to the context of personal relationship both to the one who imposed and to the one who should have suffered the punishment. The morality or otherwise of the transference of punishment depends entirely upon the wider context, both divine and human, within which it is placed.

The difficulty which arises in the application of the category of Law to the doctrine of the Atonement is not so much that it lacks elements of truth, but that it is not exhaustive. God is more than a Judge; sin is more than transgression; and man's need is for more than a new status. If a man may start from his agonizing 'threshold question,' he cannot stop there; for what is at stake is not merely release from the guilt of sin, but also rescue from its power. Indeed, if the Cross has

a cosmic as well as a human significance, it might seem
as if, left at this level, the Atonement was almost too
'parochial' in its range. Law may provide our first
clue; it can hardly be the ultimate category. Its significance is not removed; but our understanding of the
Cross must be carried to deeper levels. Perhaps what
tells most heavily against its complete adequacy is the
logical clarity and hardness of outline with which it is
normally presented. The celebrated distinction made by
Baron von Hügel between 'the clear' and 'the rich,'
which, by reason of the profundity of its subject-matter,
is incapable of coldly logical presentation without
travesty, is relevant here.[1]

Such views of the Atonement, however, possess two
abiding merits. They emphasize the Atonement as an
objective fact and assign to the Cross itself the significance of a towering and majestic peak. No reinterpretation of the Atonement which weakens or abandons
these theological achievements can claim to do justice
to its theme. Again, they call attention to an inevitable
two-sidedness within the act of redemption itself.
Here is a rescue operation undertaken on behalf of the
whole human race which must nevertheless be carried
out with full respect for the moral ordering of the
universe. Neither an inflexible severity on the part of
God which left man inextricably caught in the consequences of his own transgression, nor any method of
redemption which could be taken even by human
perversity to justify the dictum, 'God's a good fellow
and 'twill all be well,' would be consistent with the

[1] The distinction between 'the clear' and 'the rich' is utilized in Baron
F. von Hügel, *Eternal Life*.

character of God as revealed in the Bible. The action of God must at one and the same time both give to man a new status in the moral universe and reaffirm the sanctity of that moral order in the face of man's challenge and rejection. That this alone would be consistent with the will and character of God seems clear enough. That man's integrity as a moral being is also involved has not always been sufficiently observed. As the history of Calvinism shows, the Sovereignty of God and the integrity of man are paradoxically not opposites, but implicates.

CHAPTER IV

THE GUIDING CLUES: THE ETHICAL

THE second type of doctrine of the Atonement draws its master-clue from the field of ethics. Sin is regarded either as ignorance or disobedience, and the function of the Cross is conceived as the creation within redeemed man of new values.

This doctrine of the Atonement may be presented under two forms. The first may be called the Exemplarist or Moral Influence Theory, while the second is concerned with the moral obedience of Christ. The latter may take various forms. It is by far the more satisfactory, and may even with enrichments drawn from the other theories be the kind of view in which the mind can rest.

Exemplarist views stress what God has done for man in Christ. So far they might appear unexceptionable, since this is at least a major part of the standing New Testament order of priorities about the Cross. Difficulties, however, arise in the description of what God has in effect done for us in Christ. If this is conceived primarily, or even solely, in terms of the provision of a human example, this seems to come perilously near to the establishment of a theological restrictive practice. The truth for which this theory stands is that the Atonement must not merely occur; it must also be applied. The Cross is not a fact which we can take for granted, but which leaves us free to go on as we were before. The theory urges that God's forgiveness is a standing implicate of His Love, and that all that is required is that man should become forgivable through his response to that Love. Here, perhaps, we may suspect a half-truth or even the telescoping of two truths through the elimination of the middle term between them. While forgiveness is undoubtedly involved in the Love of God, the two cannot be simply identified. There is the Love of God exhibited in the eternal relationships within the Holy Trinity. Here is the fullest mutual self-donation, but it can least inadequately be described as pure joy. The fact of creation which prepares the way for the evolution of free creatures introduces at least the potentiality of suffering into that Love. Forgiveness is love operating at utmost cost to meet the predicament of human sin.[1] It is precisely this element of love operating at cost which such theories underestimate.

Again, it must be maintained that man does not become forgivable merely through his response to a human example vouchsafed through God in Christ. His plight is even more serious, and he can only become forgivable through a prior act on the part of God. Exemplarist views are rightly anxious to insist that our

[1] A distinction between the attributes of God as they are expressed within the Holy Trinity and their mode of operation seems to be involved in the very existence of a created order. The failure to make some such distinction is the principal weakness of the celebrated quotation from Mr. C. S. Dinsmore quoted, for example, in Baron von Hügel's *Essays and Addresses on the Philosophy of Religion*, II, p. 173: 'There was a cross in the heart of God before there was one planted on the green hill outside Jerusalem.'

redemption is never automatic, never transactional in a purely external way. Against any such view they would rejoice in the label, 'subjective,' often attached to them in criticism. But they tend seriously to under-estimate the extent to which God 'puts His will' into the act of Atonement. The cruciality of the Cross, its stark atrociousness, indeed the whole cost to God of the process of redemption, seem to play an inadequate part in theories of this type. Certainly this is a serious deficiency in any view which claims to offer a satisfactory account of the Atonement.

The aspect of sin upon which these theories lay most emphasis is ignorance, which is primarily dispelled by a nobler example or through access of light. Behind this view of sin lies a long historical tradition. It is more characteristic of Greek than of Hebrew ways of thinking, and has tended to recur whenever the Greek tradition became dominant in Christian theology. For different reasons it was a feature of the evolutionary optimism of the last century. Fundamentally it represents the 'light' view of sin taken by Pelagius, although (rather surprisingly) his doctrine of the Atonement does not seem to have been of the Exemplarist type.[1] If Pelagius is right as against St. Augustine in many points of detail, the latter with his 'dark' view of sin had by far the profounder insight into what it means to be a sinner. While sins of ignorance undoubtedly exist, the definition of sin as ignorance goes nowhere near the seat of the trouble.

As Bishop Kirk once pointed out, Exemplarist

[1] See the thorough study of J. Rivière in *Revue d'Histoire Ecclésiastique,* Vol. XLI (1946), pp. 5–43.

theories of the Atonement may even set an unfair premium upon certain spiritual and psychological temperaments, the emotive and mystical, as against the cold, the practical, and the phlegmatic.[1] While there may well come a time at which the Christian says to the non-Christian, 'Can't you see?' the object of vision is never simply a human warming to Christ as He hangs upon the Cross, but the acceptance of an act done for us which rescues us from a predicament from which we could not extricate ourselves. The Atonement makes us better because it saves; it does not merely save us by making us better.

Yet, if these theories are defective as an adequate account of the Atonement, at least they call attention to a necessary factor in any more adequate interpretation. If Juridical views conceive of the Cross in terms of an instrument, Exemplarist theories tend to regard it as a symbol. In reality, of course, it must be both. If redemption involves a new status before God, part at least of what it means to be a redeemed man is to accept and to implement a new set of values which flow from the Cross. But this must be regarded rather as a corollary or an application of the Atonement than as a description of the act of Atonement in itself.

The second group of views lay considerable emphasis upon the moral obedience of Christ. They are more definite and more adequate than the Exemplarist view as it is customarily presented. They may even advance beyond the merely 'subjective' into the region of 'objective' thought about the Cross. In their more balanced forms there is a double accent upon what

[1] K. E. Kirk in *Essays Catholic and Critical*, pp. 257–8.

God in Christ has done for man as well as upon what Christ as Man has wrought 'for us men and for our salvation.' Sin is regarded neither merely as ignorance to be dispelled by the provision of a more perfect example, nor even simply as the transgression of an external norm, but as rebellion against a principle which is not merely the law of God, but also the ground of man's own being.

The theory maintains that the really atoning fact was not the Cross in splendid isolation, but the Person upon the Cross in His saving totality. The death of uttermost sacrifice was matched by the life of perfect obedience, though that life would have been incomplete without death, 'even death on a cross.' It is precisely by this perfect obedience as a whole, culminating in the Cross, that the world's salvation was achieved. We knew instinctively that one major root of sin is disobedience, and here the cure matches the disease. Noble expressions of this view (in whole or part) may be found at many periods in Christian theology, and an especially notable example may be found in a document where perhaps it might least be expected, the *Bazaar of Heracleides*, probably written by Nestorius.[1] If his Christology is at least suspect, he is certainly not in error here. The cardinal importance of the obedience of Christ has been built into a number of views which (taken as a whole) might be catalogued in different ways.

Two questions seem naturally to arise, and it is upon the answer which may be returned to them that the adequacy of the theory will largely depend.

[1] Nestorius, *The Bazaar of Heracleides*. Translated and edited by G. R. Driver and L. Hodgson.

THE GUIDING CLUES: THE ETHICAL 45

1. How can a pattern of action fulfilled in the humanity of Christ be regarded as an act of God? In what sense can the moral obedience of Christ provide the conditions for an act of Divine restoration? Can the theory deal adequately with the Atonement as an act into which God puts His Will?

2. How can the moral obedience of Christ even as Man be credited and made available to disobedient humanity? Must He not simply 'deliver His own soul by His righteousness'?

The answer to these questions lies partly in the realm of Christology and partly in regions of the doctrine which we have not as yet explored.

Orthodox Christology maintains that there is a double solidarity in the Person of our Lord—His solidarity with the Father as touching His Godhead, and His solidarity with ourselves as touching His Manhood. At the Council of Chalcedon this truth was expressed by the double use of the adjective *homoousios*. The obedient Christ is the Incarnate Lord, the Son of God made Man 'for us men and for our salvation.' What He does as Man has the full authority of God behind it. 'Son though He was, yet He learned obedience through sufferings.'[1] The obedience of Christ as Man therefore extends into both spheres. From the side of God it is the expression through the Son of God made Man of the moral order against which man had rebelled and the complete fulfilment of its demands at uttermost cost. In order to reach man in his predicament of disobedience and rebellion, in an act to which God was fully committed, our Lord redresses the moral

[1] Heb. v. 8.

balance of the universe which had been disturbed by the sin of man. There is, therefore, a satisfaction involved in the Atonement, as objective theories have always maintained; but it is not directed to God's honour, as St. Anselm asserted, nor is it simply a question of the payment of a debt or even the transference of a penalty. It is written yet more deeply into the moral order of the universe against which man had offended; and its method (the restoration of disobedience through obedience) possesses a moral and spiritual cohesion which gives to the theory a certain air of inevitability. It represents precisely the kind of initiative appropriate to the God who forgives at infinite cost with full respect for the moral order of the universe of which He is alike the Source and the Guarantor.

This theory can therefore go far towards meeting the usual objections raised against 'objective' views by their 'subjective' rivals. Forgiveness won at this cost and in this realm can hardly be accused of being automatic, mechanical, or external. Although on this view redemption is primarily wrought by Christ as Man, it is not independent of the Divine Will expressed in act, for the unique Person through whom it is achieved is solid with God as well as with ourselves. Yet it also embodies the elements of truth for which the 'subjective' views themselves contend. The moral obedience of Christ inevitably points to the natural human response. Man's disobedience is cancelled by the obedience of Christ, which in turn both evokes and makes possible the renewed obedience of a redeemed humanity.

As we approach the manward implications of the theory, it is clear that the notion of example is inadequate. Happily other material is available for the purpose. There is first the Adam-Christ parallelism of the New Testament.[1] Sinful humanity is solid with Adam, and redeemed humanity is solid with Christ. As a general principle this is clear enough, though care will be needed in drawing out its further implications. The background is set out in the doctrine of the *Recapitulatio* expounded by St. Irenaeus.[2] Christ as Man has travelled the full human ground, but victoriously at every point at which man is so often defeated. There is also the more modern concept of the Representative Man, though the Christological bearing of this concept would again require somewhat careful analysis.

A starting-point may perhaps be found in the scientific concept of a test-case or a decisive experiment. Provided that it asks the right questions of its subject-matter and is performed under appropriate conditions, a scientific experiment will always prove its point. Normally it is capable of indefinite repetition, but this fact does not in itself constitute its demonstrative power. Its validity primarily depends upon its adequacy for the purposes for which it was devised. In the Incarnation we find just such a crucial experiment in the moral and spiritual spheres. On the one hand, there is a perfect calibration to the Will of God, a life of perfect obedience to the Divine Initiative; on the other hand, there is the complete testing of that obedience

[1] Rom. v. 12–21; 1 Cor. xv. 20–3, 45–9.
[2] See H. E. W. Turner, *The Patristic Doctrine of Redemption*, pp. 62–7.

by exposure to all the motives which lead to human disobedience, misunderstanding, rapid but shallow response given for the wrong reasons and on the wrong terms, treachery, blindness of heart, vested interest, injustice, cruelty, and, at the last, even death itself in a peculiarly stark and vile form. At any point retreat or disobedience might have saved Him, but, as Nestorius expressed it, 'He stood fast in thoughts of obedience.'[1] The wheel has turned full circle. The recapitulation is complete. We shall return to this analogy of the test-case at a later stage of the argument.

This crucial process of obedience to the uttermost has a double framework of reference. If, on the God-ward side, it satisfied the moral fabric of the universe because the One who fulfilled it had, as it were, the right to act on behalf of God, on the manward side, it is vicarious, because its agent was solid with ourselves, and is therefore fully accredited to act as our representative. The vicarious character of our Lord's life and death plainly emerges from the Gospels. Our Lord knew Himself to be the Suffering Servant of God in a manner which more than fulfilled the insights of Old Testament prophecy as the One who 'bore the sins of many and made intercession for the transgressors.'[2] His own commentary on the Passion spoke of the gift of His Body 'for you' and of His Blood 'poured out for many.'[3] The obedience of Christ was also for the many: 'For their sakes I sanctify Myself.'[4]

The manward implications of the saving obedience

---

[1] Nestorius, op. cit., p. 63.   [2] Isa. liii. 12.
[3] Mk. xiv. 24 (Mt. xxvi. 26–7); Lk. xxii. 19–20; 1 Cor. xi. 24.
[4] Jn. xvii. 19.

of Christ may be illustrated by the concept of the Representative Man. Here human analogies, despite their inevitable limitations, serve to make its meaning plain. The term is not simply a synonym for the ordinary man or for that half-mythical entity, the man in the street. It is usually employed to describe someone who sums up and makes articulate in word or deed the unexpressed aspirations and muddled gropings of the group which he represents. It is in this sense that during the war years Sir Winston Churchill could be called the representative Englishman. I remember seeing by the roadside in Libya a burnt-out enemy tank which bore the painted legend, 'Some chicken, some neck.' In this way an unknown British soldier found his thoughts and feelings mirrored in the speeches of a representative Englishman. This is a very faint and imperfect analogy to the sense in which our Lord is revealed in the Gospels as the Representative Man. In considering Him mankind sees what humanity itself was intended to become and what through its own disobedience it has failed to be. Is this perhaps something of the overtone which the Fourth Evangelist detects behind Pilate's words at the trial, 'Behold the Man,' 'Behold your King'?

Representative men on the stage of history are normally confined to a given setting or a particular epoch. Only the very greatest are capable of being, as it were, carried over beyond their immediate environment. But the Christ who is our Representative is, in fact, ageless. His immediate historical setting, from which it would be theologically wrong as well as historically idle to try to detach Him, was the world

D

of a Galilean countryman of the first Christian century. But the content of His earthly life is so closely related to the basic realities of all human existence that it is still possible to regard Him as our Representative under the very different outward circumstances of the technological civilization of the twentieth century. His Lordship of human life is one and indivisible through the ages; it is only the idiom in which it is expressed and the conditions under which it must be realized which change from generation to generation. Because Christ is our Representative as Man, His action can be vicarious. The predicament in which we are caught as men was in its essential ingredients the context in which His obedience was worked out even to the death.

But there is still a further step to be taken. Christ's obedience can, it seems, avail for our disobedience. It can be significantly described as vicarious. But can it heal our disobedience by being transmitted to us? Here the concept of an inclusive humanity requires some discussion. As we have seen, the New Testament notes the parallel between solidarity in Adam and solidarity in Christ. So far as Adam is concerned, one classical form of the theory is that of seminal identity. While this is never explicitly stated by St. Paul, it is adumbrated in a wholly different context by the author of the Epistle to the Hebrews.[1] Difficulties certainly arise

---

[1] The question of Pauline exegesis turns upon the meaning of ἐφ'ᾧ in Romans v. 12. This is normally taken to mean 'because' or 'inasmuch as.' The Latin versions read *in quo* which is ambiguous and might be interpreted in terms of seminal identity. See W. Sanday and A. C. Headlam, *Romans* (I.C.C.), pp. 133–4, and C. H. Dodd, *Romans* (Moffatt Commentary), pp. 78–80. In Hebrews vii. 5 the concept of seminal identity is quite clear.

over the question of the historico-temporal existence of Adam. As it stands it can scarcely be extended to cover our solidarity with our Lord. Yet, as Adam is the representative head of fallen humanity, in a far truer and more mystical sense our Lord is the Representative Head of redeemed and restored humanity. It has been truly said that we are 'sons in the Son'; yet we are not sons as the Son, for He is by nature what we are only by adoption and grace. There are differences to be safeguarded as well as identities to be observed. Since He is our Representative Man, His moral obedience may be described as vicarious; but since He is also the beginning of a new humanity, spiritually reborn and ethically refashioned in Him, His obedience is capable of extension into redeemed lives. Thus the moral obedience of Christ has, in effect, a triple framework of reference. Objectively it is God's act in Christ satisfying the demands of the moral universe; subjectively it is Christ's act as Man, which not only vicariously annuls our disobedience, but is also capable of being spiritually re-enacted within us. Thus it can not only annul but also heal our disobedience, and so provide a double answer to the rebellion which is one principal root of our sin. Here the fact of 'Christ for us' is reinforced by the experience of 'Christ within us,' though we should do well to resist any temptation to telescope these two aspects of the Atonement. It is, however, the merit of theories of the Atonement which are sometimes described as mystical that they take full account of this further stage in our understanding of our redemption.

CHAPTER V

THE GUIDING CLUES: THE PSYCHOLOGICAL

IT is wholly natural that an important contemporary line of approach to the Atonement should be through the medium of psychology. The old and (as some would have us believe) the classical theory of vicarious victory may be removed from its original setting and reinterpreted in terms of release from sin and the resolution of inner conflict. The sin of which it is the remedy is conceived in terms of inner frustration and disintegration, and it may be suggested that (for this view) one principal effect of the Atonement is the provision of a new focus for living, leading to the new man in Christ Jesus.

If the reading be correct, the writer to the Hebrews speaks of the 'contradiction of sinners against themselves.'[1] But whether this is his original meaning or not, it is undeniably true that sin is self-contradiction. It is the type of behaviour which cannot lead to life or freedom. Deliberate persistence in known sin eats deeply into the roots of the personality, and leads first to frustration and finally to the disintegration of the self. The logical result of the failure to call things by their proper names and to deal with them at their true level simply pushes them below the level of consciousness and leads to trouble which is more widely diffused

---

[1] Heb. xii. 3.

and more deep-seated. The acute analysis of anxiety, especially in its pathological forms, in such a book as Paul Tillich's *The Courage to Be* is an up-to-date commentary on sin as frustration. The concept of guilt, which in Christian usage is firmly attached to personal accountability before God, significantly persists in the vocabulary of the modern psychologist, though it is often interpreted in an entirely different sense. Even when removed from its Godward reference and removed from the region of conscious choice, the phenomenon of guilt remains a constant factor in human experience.

This diagnosis of the nature of sin is sufficiently grave, and is at least more profound than some which we have previously examined. By contrast, the description of sin as ignorance seems incurably superficial. It is, however, exposed to one serious limitation. It seems to approach sin by way of its more depressing human consequences rather than of its primary standard of reference to God Himself. The effects of sin in some individual human lives are, no doubt, faithfully depicted; the hard core of the problem may lie elsewhere. Again, while the Atonement certainly has important corollaries in the inner life of the self, we must beware even of appearing to regard redemption as primarily good psychiatry.

The doctrine of the Atonement which may most readily be associated with this aspect of man's predicament is the theory of vicarious victory. This has been studied at close quarters by two Swedish scholars, Bishop Aulén and Dr. Leivestad, though the claims

which have been made on its behalf may be somewhat
exaggerated.[1] In its classical form the theory is associated with the victory of our Lord over the demonic
powers.

There is abundant evidence that the world into which
our Lord came believed strongly in the existence of
powers of a supernatural order. Within Judaism the
Apocalyptic Movement in particular reflected a widen-
ing belief both in angels and demons, while a kind of
planetary determinism represented a familiar tenet in
many Gentile circles. The evidence of the Gospels
strongly suggests that our Lord shared the belief of His
day in these supernatural powers, whether under divine
control or consciously in revolt from God. The healing
miracles, especially the cure of those who were or who
believed themselves to be under the control of demons,
were marks of the new age which He came to bring.
The entrance of the kingdom of God into the world
bore witness to a 'strong man bound.'[2] The temptations of our Lord are related as a series of conflicts
with an external tempter and St. Luke adds the
significant note that 'the devil departed from Him for
a season.' A hint of the type of occasion upon which
the conflict was renewed is given in the stinging rebuke
to St. Peter, 'Get thee behind Me, Satan,' in response to
the shocked protest of the Apostle which greeted the
first prediction of the Passion. The Agony in the

[1] See G. Aulén, *Christus Victor*, and R. Leivestad, *Christ the Con-
queror*. I have reviewed the Patristic section of Bishop Aulén's book
in my *Patristic Doctrine of Redemption*, pp. 47–69.
[2] Mk. iii. 27; Mt. xii. 29; Lk. xi. 21.

Garden of Gethsemane is also interpreted as a further temptation to evade the Cross.[1]

St. Paul clearly shared contemporary belief to the full. Indeed, to the normally accepted cosmic powers he adds what might be described as the Pauline irregulars, Sin and Death. He speaks of the Cross itself as the supreme occasion of our Lord's victory over the forces which were ranged against Him. They are the world-rulers who acted in ignorance, 'otherwise they would not have crucified the Lord of glory.'[2] While we cannot altogether exclude human rulers like Pilate, Caiaphas, and Herod from our exegesis of the text, it seems altogether more probable that St. Paul had more mysterious elemental forces in his mind here.[3]

The early Fathers extended the canvas without notably improving the picture. Accepting the same cosmology, they interpreted the main events in our Lord's life in terms of victory over the demons even in cases where the Gospels were silent. Thus, for example, the Virgin Birth was regarded in some circles as a successful attempt to break through a *cordon insanitaire* of demons intended to prevent the Incarnation and the Ascension as a return to heavenly places despite similar opposition in the same quarters.[4]

There is little doubt that this New Testament and

[1] Mk. i. 12–13; Mt. iv. 1–11; Lk. iv. 1–13 (Q). Cp. also Mk. viii. 31–3; Mt. xvi. 22–3; Mk. xiv. 32–42; Mt. xxvi. 36–46; Lk. xxii. 40–6 (especially verse 43).

[2] 1 Cor. ii. 8.

[3] See C. Anderson Scott, *Christianity according to St. Paul*, pp. 28–38.

[4] See Martin Werner, *The Formation of Christian Dogma*, pp. 95–106, and my summary of selected material bearing on the subject in *The Patristic Doctrine of Redemption*, pp. 49–53.

Patristic background to the doctrine of the Atonement reads somewhat strangely to many modern Christians. We do not believe in the existence of these demonic powers, at least not with the New Testament level of intensity. In countries which have been nominally Christian for many centuries, with a long record of Christian worship and practice behind them, we are accustomed to think of our world as a 'tame world' in which there has been a cumulative victory for Christ. A closer analogy to the New Testament situation comes from the mission field, where the new convert finds the need for deliverance from a whole atmosphere or style of living which has not yet been baptized into Christ. There may well be a theological as well as a social and political significance to be found in the Mau Mau movement in Kenya. Perhaps, too, we tend to exaggerate the tameness of our own world and forget the forces of retrogression which lie beneath the surface. The real question is how far below the surface they really lie.

On this whole question contemporary theology seems to speak with two voices. The question may, for example, seriously be raised whether or not our Lord's belief in the existence of demonic powers forms part of His human historical conditioning, or whether the demon-possessed would now be diagnosed by modern medicine as more or less acute cases of schizophrenia. If Dr. Hodgson claims that 'our progress in the scientific control of nature which leads us to disregard the activities of devils, is one of the ways in which God is enlisting our co-operation in rescuing His world from their control,' in other words, an extension of the area of human rationality, Professor C. S. Lewis would seek to convince us that the virtual cessation of belief in the demonic is in itself a device of the devil.[1] The 'mystery of iniquity' must certainly not be set too low.[2]

Yet, even if we leave aside the problem whether we are theologically justified in 'demythologizing' this theory with any degree of completeness, it is clear that it contains much that can be profitably applied to the life of the individual.

The victory of Christ won for us through His Life, Death, and Resurrection taken together must clearly be applied to the individual life, which has no power of itself to help itself. The decisive victory over sin has been won objectively in a redemptive pattern of action which saves us not only from the guilt of sin, but also from its power. But it also needs to be implemented or worked out subjectively in human lives which are in process of being redeemed. Thus, once again, 'Christ for us' is reinforced by 'Christ in us,' as His power, released through His Death and Resurrection, passes into us and strengthens our weakness. Professor Hodges rightly recalls an old phrase, 'the winning power of Christ,' though I venture to think that he restricts it too narrowly to the Exemplarist view.[3]

It may further be suggested that one important aspect of the Atonement which this application of the doctrine of vicarious victory to the individual life brings to light is the provision of a new focus round which the sinful personality with its divided will can be re-orientated. This is certainly implied in a familiar passage from the

[1] L. Hodgson, *The Doctrine of the Atonement*, p. 49; C. S. Lewis, *Screwtape Letters*, pp. 39–40.   [2] 2 Thess. ii. 7.
[3] H. A. Hodges, *The Pattern of Atonement*, p. 40.

Epistle to the Hebrews, 'Looking unto Jesus the author and finisher of our faith; who for the joy which was set before Him endured the Cross, despising the shame, and hath set down at the right hand of the throne of God.'[1] The new focus is plainly linked with the decisive action of our Lord, the victory of the Cross won once for all time and ratified by His heavenly session at the right hand of God. As man learns to look away from himself and to our Lord, so the benefits of Christ's Passion become operative within him and his own personality becomes unified and remade in Christ.

While this insight into the significance of the Cross has undoubted truth, and possesses considerable relevance for some aspects of contemporary life, it may be doubted whether it can stand in isolation as an adequate account of the Cross. If the Atonement has important implications in the field of psychology, it is clearly far more than a helpful spiritual technique for the defeated and divided. Vicarious victory (with or without its mythological trappings) is not restricted to the confines of the human self. But what tells most heavily against the adequacy of this view is the description of sin in terms of its human effects rather than from the standpoint of our relationship to God Himself. Although the theory may well speak to some aspects of our condition, there are yet further steps towards the understanding of the Cross which still need to be taken. The clue of psychology may be better adapted to illuminate some implications of human sin than to lay bare its very heart.

[1] Heb. xii. 2.

CHAPTER VI

THE GUIDING CLUES: THE PERSONAL

AN objector might well take exception to the choice of the term 'personal' as the heading for this part of our discussion. He might reasonably urge that ethics is concerned with the guiding principles of a particular set of personal relations, while psychology represents the scientific investigation of human personality as such. But the reasons which have led to the selection of these terms are wholly different. The designation 'ethical' is here applied to theories of the Atonement which discover its meaning in the provision of new moral and spiritual values, while the psychological approach to the doctrine emphasizes the release from inner tension and the answer to some of the more devastating consequences of human sin offered to man through the Cross. On the other hand, the term 'personal' focuses attention not upon the human effects of sin, but upon its power to cause a breach of personal relationship to God, and upon the restoration of that relationship in Christ.

Here once again we are brought closely into touch with New Testament terms and images. Sin is conceived as estrangement which makes us aliens and strangers from God.[1] Instead of being free-born sons in our Father's house, we know ourselves to be wander-

[1] Eph. ii. 11–22.

ing prodigals. We have lost the sense of being at home with God. Man's deepest need in his sinful predicament is reconciliation to God.[1] In the Epistle to the Hebrews the fruits of Christ's Redemption are described as 'entrance into the holiest by a new and living way.'[2] St. Paul expresses the same idea no less graphically as 'access' or 'boldness.'[3] A new road to God has been opened for man through the redeeming death of Christ.

It is clear that the conception of sin as estrangement, the barrier to a free and unimpeded relationship to God, penetrates far more deeply into its nature than anything which we have so far considered. Yet it is by no means inconsistent with the aspects of its nature and consequences which have been noted in previous chapters. The idea of sin as transgression discloses one main cause of estrangement, the breach of a known norm, though it is here seen in the light of a relationship to the God of whose will it is the expression. The rebellion of which other theories speak is no longer restricted to the relation between a subject and his king; it must be reinterpreted to provide for the bond which exists between a father and a son or between friends. The frustration which sin brings in its train is now seen to be the consequence of the loss of the supreme experience of which man is capable, communion with God.

In the sphere of human relationships we can discover reliable analogies to the concept of sin as estrangement,

[1] Rom. v. 10; 2 Cor. v. 18–20; Col. i. 20–1; Eph. ii. 16.

[2] Heb. x. 19–20.

[3] 'Access' ($\pi\rho\sigma\alpha\gamma\omega\gamma\dot\eta$), Rom. v. 2; Eph. ii. 18, iii. 12; 'Boldness' ($\pi\alpha\rho\rho\eta\sigma\dot\iota\alpha$), Eph. iii. 12; cp. Heb. x. 19.

and even some faint resemblance to the process of reconciliation. As we have already seen, broken relationships can always be traced to some action which has set up a barrier between the people concerned, or (changing the metaphor slightly) to conduct which has started a breach between them. The initial cause may not appear serious in itself; indeed, it may even be wholly or largely imaginary. But once it has occurred it cannot simply be ignored or treated as if it did not exist. Unreconciled breaches merely widen in the course of time. So over the centuries the power of human sin to estrange from God has accumulated with devastating effect. Again, in human life the initiative rests most appropriately with the one to whom the injury has been done, although cases may sometimes occur in which the first step is taken by the wrong-doer. Here the analogy is somewhat defective, for Christians know that the initiative in their reconciliation lies (and can only lie) with God. In a breach of human relations there will normally be faults on both sides; offence can be taken as well as given. But the New Testament always seems to speak of our reconciliation to God as a unilateral process, and never uses the language of the second Anglican article, 'to reconcile the Father to us.' It may, however, be suspected that the authors of the article were telescoping into a single brief phrase ideas which, although found in the New Testament in isolation, are not normally associated with each other. As we have already seen, God's reconciliation of the sinner cannot be based upon principles which might even appear to countenance the conduct which has led to the breach.

Restoration of fellowship, whether with God or among men, can only be at cost. Here no force is more creative or more potent in its effects than vicarious suffering. In human relationships no less than in God's dealings with men, to love is to suffer, and to suffer is to love. Finally, a new and permanent relationship can only be established if the evil can in some way be made redemptive or turned into good. A marriage which has experienced a radical and thoroughgoing restoration, or what Roman Catholic moral theologians describe as a *sanatio in integrum*, becomes more deeply and truly a marriage than if it had pursued the even tenor of its ways untried. The evil remains evil in itself, but evil transformed by being made the occasion of forgiveness and reconciliation makes new ranges of living possible. Here is a further analogy to the Christian experience of reconciliation.

Extreme care must, of course, be taken over the way in which this paradoxical fact is expressed. The danger of false deductions reduces St. Paul in a well-known passage to a series of indignant glottal stops.[1] Yet he cannot do justice to the spiritual experience of being remade in Christ without recourse to this paradox. The fact of his conversion on the Damascus road, in which he was, as it were, 'put under close arrest' by the Risen Lord, and where his life was 'gripped once for all by Jesus Christ,' is never far from the surface of his mind.[2] Saul, the persecutor of the infant Church, becomes, by the grace of God, Paul, the Apostle to the

[1] Rom. iii. 1–8.
[2] Phil. iii. 12: the word rendered 'apprehended' in the English versions.

Gentiles; and it might well appear that he might never have become the one without having been the other. St. Augustine penitent may even be capable of greater heights of Christian spirituality than St. Augustine innocent. Yet it is only from within the Christian experience of forgiveness that language of this kind can ever be used at all. What is involved here is not the weakening of the moral law and its demands, but a wondering recognition of the way in which God meets man in his predicament and makes the causes of his estrangement the raw material of his restoration.

How, then, does the Cross fulfil this pattern of reconciliation? The barriers erected against God by man's sin are certainly not imaginary. The argument of previous chapters will have entirely failed in its purpose if they are not seen to be grimly real. Man's natural heritage is a race-history of alienation from God, and his own unaided efforts can only serve to deepen this estrangement. The first healing steps which make reconciliation possible cannot come from the rebel and the stranger. The reconciling initiative can only come from the side of God.

God draws the sting of sin by exposing Himself in the Person of His Son to its full consequences, and by turning the Cross, the fitting symbol of man's rebellion and estrangement, into the very instrument of our redemption. What more could man do to display his rejection of God than to crucify God's Son and his own representative? What more could God do to effect man's reconciliation to Himself than to transform this same crowning act of rejection into the instrument of forgiving and restoring Love? The Lament over

Jerusalem, the Cry of Dereliction, the Word of Forgiveness, and the triumphant 'It is finished' are the appropriate commentary on this pattern of reconciliation.[1] It is, as it were, the Parables of the Lost Coin, the Lost Sheep, and the Lost Son blended into one, and seen in the light of their inevitable corollary, the Cross. For the Cross is the implicate in action of what the parables express at the level of symbol and image. Here all the motives which lead to a breach of relationship on the human plane meet and are directed against One who is alike the Incarnate Son of God and our own Representative, who under the conditions of a perfect manhood, lived in full and unbroken fellowship with the Father. Only so could the cost of a restored relationship be borne by God; only so could the power of human sin to estrange and separate be fully accepted by God, and transformed into the means of the salvation of the world. While forgiveness was eternally implicit in the Love of God, the Cross became the fitting instrument through which that forgiveness was actualized to the sons of men. Here the Love of God takes the initiative at infinite cost to break down the consequences of man's rebellion through the power of suffering, and to restore him to fellowship with Himself.

But if reconciliation involves a unilateral act for which God in Christ has made the fullest provision, the restored relationship to which it leads is inevitably two-sided. Through the healing power of the Cross our communion with God, increasingly lost through our sin, becomes progressively restored in Christ. The

[1] Mt. xxiii. 37; Lk. xiii. 34 (Q); Mk. xv. 34; Mt. xxvii. 46; Lk. xxii. 34; Jn. xix. 30.

initiative which draws man back to Himself remains with God, but the prodigal must come to his senses and return from the far country into which his sin has driven him. A 'new and living way' has been opened through the Cross, but God and man must henceforth travel it together, and in the course of the journey there emerges the new man in Christ.

E

CHAPTER VII

THE COSMIC SIGNIFICANCE OF THE CROSS

By reason of his special position within creation, man finds himself impelled to raise ultimate questions about the universe in which he is placed. Is it hostile, friendly, or merely indifferent to his purposes? Can he find himself at home in the universe, or is he living 'stranger and afraid in a world he never made'? Is his best hope to seek for himself an oasis of security in a notably insecure world, perhaps an ivory tower or, more nobly, a neat and tidy garden in the midst of a surrounding wilderness? Or is there such a thing as living with or against the grain of the universe?

And all the time man knows himself to be part of the question mark which he sets against his world. He has within himself a double striving. On the one hand, he seeks for his own independence, the denial and transcendence of his creatureliness, while, on the other hand, he knows his dependence, immediately upon others and ultimately upon God. His desire to be alone is balanced by his fear of being alone. In these circumstances it appears natural to speak of sin as disorder.

Here again the Cross speaks to his condition, for the Atonement has a cosmic setting without which it might almost appear parochial in its range. It is, as Oliver Quick has described it, the 'Gospel of the New World.'

At this point, however, it might be objected that Christian theology has overreached itself. In philosophy, metaphysics has for some time past been on the defensive, and many philosophers have preferred to devote their attention to close linguistic analysis. These are, no doubt, technical questions which really demand technical answers. On the other hand, Christian theology, just because of its subject-matter, has never been afraid to push its questions to the very limits to which the human mind can stretch. Yet at its best it has always had a careful eye for the type of answer which it might expect to find. It has not sought to impose theoretical answers upon questions which only admit of treatment along different lines. And it has never been afraid to invoke the method of faith, with its corollary of committed living, where the nature of the inquiry appeared to demand it. Rightly understood, faith is neither blind nor lacking in reasonable ground; it can, however, transcend the step-by-step logicalities of unaided human thought, and thus find solutions which are not available to the methods of philosophy. Divine action on the one hand and committed human living on the other form a coherent approach to the ultimate problems of the universe.

These preliminary considerations are exceedingly relevant to our understanding of the Atonement. A world in which the Cross and Resurrection of Jesus Christ have occurred can never be the same again. It is a world which must be valued in a radically different way. The moral law is not merely a set of human conventions or a code of conduct against which man has transgressed; it is a reflexion of the character of

God and the most readily legible part of His signature in the created order. That God Himself in Christ, acting decisively for man's redemption, should respect its conditions and satisfy its requirements, is in itself the surest guarantee that it is no interloper in the universe. The new human values to which we are committed by the Cross are living 'with the grain' and not 'against the grain' of the universe. Further, if the Cross itself is part of the warp and woof of the universe, then the moral order itself is not simply a norm of inflexible severity, the means whereby 'the many are constituted sinners'; it is itself taken up into the redemptive purposes of God. Seen in the light of the Cross, the moral order does not merely declare us sinners, it also provides for forgiven men.

Here, too, the vicarious victory of our Lord is to be seen in its fullest light. So far we have come to understand it as a method of dealing radically and powerfully with our own inner contradictions and frustrations. In greater harmony with its original background, it can also be interpreted as a victory of cosmic proportions. It is concerned with the question of the supremacy of good or of evil in the universe.

The analogy of the test-case or the scientific experiment has already been used to shed some light upon the redemptive significance of our Lord's humanity. But it may also prove possible to extend its application tentatively into more mysterious regions of the Divine purpose. In the field of relativity the presuppositions of the new theory were confirmed by the Michelson-Morley experiment, which yielded a consistently negative result under test conditions. The phenomena, interrogated in this particular way, refused to behave as they should have done if the older account of time and space had been true. The groundwork of the theory had, of course, been worked out before this decisive test was applied. We may not be wholly in error in conceiving a somewhat similar situation with regard to the Cross. Here, under test conditions, which included the character and Person of the Incarnate Subject, the motives of human rejection to which He was exposed and the stark atrocity of the death demanded of Him, is a crucial experiment in which either God or evil must prevail. Here (if anywhere) the sovereignty of God must be discredited and evil enthroned. Indeed (apart from one Word from the Cross), on the evening of the first Good Friday the victory of evil might well have seemed complete. But beyond the Cross stands the empty tomb, and man's final word of rejection is matched by God's acceptance of the worst that man could do, and its transformation into the means of man's redemption. Man's 'No' was answered by God's 'Yes.' The victory of God and the defeat of evil, crucially tested, were henceforth complete.

But this victory, even though it took place in time and space, is not simply a transcript of human history. It effected man's salvation, but it has more than simply a human reference. For it has shown that the principle of suffering and forgiving love, the initiative of love operating at cost, is part of the 'grain' of the universe. The Cross has light to shed upon God's creation as a whole, and not merely upon man's redemption. The new human values to which the Cross commits us are not merely a subjective 'warming' to the Person of the

Crucified; they are deeply written into the fabric of the universe, and our justification for making this seemingly daring act of faith is derived from the fact that they are here embodied and illustrated in Divine action.

Even more mysteriously St. Paul speaks as if the whole created order partakes in its own measure in the redemptive work of Christ. 'For the earnest expectation of creation waiteth for the revealing of the sons of God. For creation was subjected to vanity, not of its own will, but by reason of Him who subjected it, in the hope that creation itself also shall be delivered from the bondage of corruption into the glorious liberty of the children of God. For we know that the whole creation groaneth and travaileth in pain together until now.'[1]

Here Quick warns us that we must tread carefully.[2] To confuse evil and finitude would be to fall into the cardinal error of philosophical Monism. To be a creature and to be a rebellious creature are not identical propositions. There is a further danger of the 'pathetic fallacy,' the overspill of concepts and value-judgements from human into sub-human forms of life. A geologist studies the 'faults' which disturb the symmetry of the earth's surface, but his use of the term is entirely free from the taint of culpability which belongs to the word as applied to human actions. A surgeon can speak of a 'malignant growth' without any hint of malice afore-thought. Suffering in animals does not appear to possess either the same quality or the same texture as human pain. The 'pathetic fallacy' involves either a misuse of categories or even an unperceived change in

[1] Rom. viii. 19–22.
[2] O. C. Quick, *The Gospel of the New World*, pp. 15–33.

the question under discussion. Yet the universe is all of one piece, although it operates at different levels corresponding to the principal stages of the *scala naturae* or the evolutionary process. Each appears to build upon its predecessors, and is characterized by an increasing richness of content and complexity of response to environment. Again, each, as the Christian believes, marks a new stage in the unfolding of God's creation. Man is organic to the universe, and the universe is organic to man. Is St. Paul, then, too daring in his claim that the redemptive activity of God extends into every region of the created order?

Yet, despite the wide sweep of his thought in this passage, it is important to note what he does and what he does not say. He speaks not of 'evil,' but of 'vanity' or 'futility.' Is this perhaps a hint of the seemingly wasteful prodigality of nature to which natural selection is the modern scientific equivalent? The phrase 'the bondage of corruption' is, no doubt, to be understood in the light of the close connexion which he habitually traces between sin and death, though significantly enough he avoids the direct use of either term. The bare allusion to the fact of pain does not enable us to judge how far, if at all, he has succumbed to the 'pathetic fallacy.'

The existence of evil and of suffering remain the two major problems in the interpretation of the universe. Evil is certainly a surd, an irrational factor in human life; but its correlation with human and like intelligence endowed with the power of choice and self-determination at least serves to limit the field of exploration. In any case, its fundamental character is more truly

revealed in its fatal capacity to alienate man from God
than in its irrationality. Paradoxically, however, the
problem of suffering is more difficult to handle, owing
to its occurrence in the universe at levels to which the
categories of intelligence and conscious choice are not
as yet applicable. It is, however, probable that a world
in which evil existed without suffering would be an even
more difficult world for which to offer any reasonable
explanation. While emphasis has been laid upon the
power of suffering love to transform and redeem, there
are other aspects of suffering which tell in the opposite
direction. For it can also serve to distort human attitudes and judgements, and to turn the personality of
the sufferer in upon itself. It is surprising how large a
space in the world of an individual can be taken up by
an aching tooth or an arthritic joint. The problem of
suffering remains acute precisely because of its occurrence in contexts in which its use for the purposes of
a consciously shared redemption cannot readily be
imagined.

There is certainly no theoretical or academic answer
to these two problems, even on Christian premises, still
less if we fail to take the specifically Christian subject-
matter into account. For we should then be faced with
two possibilities. Either we must abandon (prematurely,
as the Christian believes) the attempt to make the fullest
possible sense of our universe, or (if we make the
existence of evil and suffering a key-feature in our
interpretation of the universe) we are left with an even
more formidable problem on our hands, the problem
of good.

Yet in both cases God's action in Christ provides

something different, and something better, than an academic answer. To meet the problem of evil, God offers to man a redemption grounded in human history and yet with cosmic implications of the highest order. Through the victory of the Cross, evil has been shown in its true colours as an intruder into the created order and a pretender to the throne of the universe. By the same Cross, the sting of suffering, which lies in its power to distort human life and to wall off the sufferer from God and his neighbour, has also been drawn. For the Cross reveals that the Divine initiative has, surprisingly enough, taken the form of suffering. God in Christ has accepted suffering, and not only triumphed over it, but also made it the means of breaking through the fact and the consequences of man's estrangement from Himself. And St. Paul goes even further, and includes the whole of creation in its own measure within the scope of the redemptive action of God. The selection of suffering as the medium of the Divine Initiative must clearly determine our estimate of its significance, wherever it is found.

There is, however, a further factor in the distinctively Christian approach to evil and suffering God's action, and man's response in committed living, form two components within a single framework. These virtually represent the elements of truth for which the objective and subjective theories of the Atonement have contended. We have already seen that they are, in fact, complementary to each other.

The situation with regard to suffering is rather more complex, although the same framework can be traced even here. The Christian is deeply committed to the task of preventing and relieving suffering, by every means in his power. Yet at the same time, as far as suffering falls to his lot, and can neither be remedied nor avoided, he learns to accept it in the light of the Cross, refusing to allow it to engross his attention or to limit his perspective, and using it redemptively as occasion serves. This double approach of removal and acceptance distinguishes the Christian attitude to suffering from its principal rivals. The humanitarian concentrates upon its removal, while certain types of mystic appear to confine themselves to acceptance. The moment of acceptance in this sense is inevitably missing in principle from the Christian approach to evil. Once again St. Paul places the emphasis precisely where we should expect to find it. 'Revelation' on God's side is matched by 'hope' on man's side. Neither God's action nor man's response is neglected in the passage under discussion.

There remains, however, a final difficulty. To speak of a 'redeemed world,' and to point to a decisive victory of God won over evil and suffering in Christ, raises in an acute form the problem of world disorder continuing. St. Paul shows himself already aware of this difficulty. 'The whole creation groaneth and travaileth in pain together until now, and not only so, but ourselves also, which have the first-fruits of the Spirit, even we ourselves groan within ourselves, waiting for our adoption, namely, the redemption of our body.'[1] Even redeemed man, who has already received the well-springs of a renewed humanity, still awaits its full and final completion in hope. Both St. Paul and the writer to the

[1] Rom. viii. 22–3.

Hebrews apply the words of the Psalmist, 'Thou hast put all things in subjection under his feet,' to the redemptive victory of the Son of Man, and for both it is a present fact with a future consummation. 'For He must reign until He hath put all things under His feet'; 'For now we see not yet all things subjected to Him, but we see Jesus crowned with glory and honour.'[1] There is a certain ambivalence about the cosmic victory of the Cross which makes it necessary to speak of it in eschatological terms. But this is a phenomenon which also underlies other departments of Christian existence. It is the nerve of the long-standing dispute over the exegesis of the phrase 'the kingdom of God' between the two schools of futurist and realized eschatology, in which it seems as if both sides have proved their point without being able to exclude that of their opponents. It explains the inevitable two-sidedness of Christian baptism which exposes us to the paradoxical appeal to 'become what we are.' Through the Cross we are already living in a redeemed world, but that redemption is neither completely revealed in the present world-order nor fully realized in ourselves.

The parallel drawn in another connexion by Cullmann between the respective roles of V-Day and D-Day in the late war is relevant here.[2] The decisive engagement (of which it is true that to fail here is to fail everywhere) has already been fought, and victory achieved; but the whole campaign has not yet been brought to a successful conclusion. 'Mopping up operations,' some of considerable magnitude, still

[1] Ps. viii. 6, quoted in 1 Cor. xv. 24–8 and Heb. ii. 8.
[2] O. Cullmann, *Christ and Time*, p. 84 and elsewhere.

remain. From the side of God, the world is already a
redeemed world; those who share in the fruits of His
redemption know themselves already to be living in
such a world. But from man's side, the battle still
rages hotly. This is part of the relative cosmic dualism
which Bishop Aulén finds so characteristic of classical
Christian theology.[1] The Christian finds himself to be
engaged in a life-and-death struggle of which the
ultimate issue is not for one moment in doubt. Both
sides of this paradox must be held with equal intensity.
If this seems intolerable, it is perhaps worth noticing
that it cannot simply be evaded by ceasing to hold the
Christian faith; it is also to be found in Communism,
which teaches the inevitability of certain economic and
social trends, and yet demands the Communist equivalent of committed and consecrated living to achieve its
purposes. Thus both Christian and secular eschatology
have a similar sense of 'living in the overlap of the
ages.'

It would be as untrue to ignore what has already been
accomplished on God's side as to be blind to what still
remains to be achieved on man's side. Already, in
principle and in actuality (God's actuality), since the
Cross and Resurrection of our Lord, suffering and
forgiving love, love operating at cost, has been vindicated as the principle which the moral order of the
universe not only accepts, but upon which it is already
constructed. How man is to appropriate and to respond
to the forgiving love of God will next claim our
attention.

[1] G. Aulén, *Christus Victor*, especially pp. 75 and 170.

CHAPTER VIII

GOD'S INITIATIVE AND MAN'S RESPONSE

THE final stage of our inquiry into the meaning of the Cross will be concerned with the main problems involved in what might be called the application of the Atonement to human life. It will, however, be necessary first to review briefly the conclusions which have so far suggested themselves with regard to the two complementary truths, for which the objective and subjective theories have classically stood, God's initiative and man's response.

God's initiative takes place in action or, paradoxically, in suffering. The charge of Sabellianism which might be raised against such a statement is adequately met by the qualification that this suffering is centred in the Person of the Incarnate Lord. His whole earthly life, rising to its climax in His Death and Resurrection, forms a pattern of action in which the moral order of the universe, challenged to the point of rebellion by man's sin, is satisfied or vindicated. This is the truth embodied in Juridical views, although the analogy of Law seems inadequate to express the full truth which they seek to convey. Something more is involved in man's sin than the transgression of an external norm externally and impersonally applied. For the moral law is both the reflexion of the character of God and the principle of cohesion of man's own being. Since it is also the most important clue to man's understanding of his universe, the moral law may even be described as possessing a cosmic reference. The sin of man is therefore more than transgression, more even than rebellion leading to personal frustration and even disintegration; it is the symptom of an even more deepseated disorder. It puts him 'out of sorts' with the universe and, above all, breaks his fellowship with God. In this particular sequence of events in history, God, in His quest for man, has wrought man's forgiveness in the only way which would not merely set aside the moral order but also vindicate it against man's rebellious challenge. God takes and retains the initiative by suffering, in and through His Son, the full effects of man's challenge, and triumphs over them. Here is part, at least, of the truth of the theory of vicarious victory, stripped of its surface mythology.

But this rescue-operation is not merely a transaction even on the widest possible scale. Man's rebellion is not an entity which can, as it were, be objectified into a thing in itself. It has no meaning apart from rebellious people or personal rebels. This implies not only beings condemned by their own act to frustration or worse, but persons in need of reconciliation to the source of their own being, who is Himself richly and profoundly personal. The Atonement represents the restoration of personal relationship at infinite cost on the initiative of the God who has been wronged. God in Christ draws the sting of man's rebellion and sterilizes it of its power to fester and decay. More even than that, by coming down into a test-situation created and defined by man's sin, God in Christ makes it the raw material of reconciliation and the instrument of His redemption. A thoroughgoing restoration of man's relationship to God takes place through the medium of his crowning act of rebellion. God's 'Yes' is unalterably superimposed upon man's 'No.'

Yet, if without God's initiative we could not be redeemed, it is also clear that God will not redeem us without ourselves. The pattern of suffering and redemptive love safeguards, as nothing else could, the creaturely freedom which man has misused as the springboard for most uncreaturely rebellion. Restoration and recreation follow the same principles as the order of creation. Man's response is as much part of the story of redemption as God's initiative. The crisis of redemption from God's side must be implemented in the manward process of being redeemed. Here four elements seem to be involved. There is first a new status before God. We are henceforth 'accepted in the Beloved.'[1] Without this new status the redeemed life would be impossible. There are new values. The selfishness inherent in rebellion is seen to be the ethical 'lie in the soul'; it is to live 'against the grain' of the moral universe. Through the Cross love is enthroned above selfishness, and suffering may not only be bravely borne and objectively carried (as, for example, by Socrates); it can also be used redemptively. This ethical revaluation involves a new focus for human personality. The ingrained egocentricity of selfishness is corrected by the reorientation of the personality round a new centre. This results from a new relationship to God. Man is no longer the rebel and the

[1] Eph. i. 6.

stranger, but offers the response of a renewed obedience to the reconciling initiative of God. He remains a creature, but he is no longer an estranged creature. He becomes, in fact, a new man.

Both aspects of the Atonement, God's initiative and man's response, meet in Christ. It is in the Person of the Incarnate Lord that the drama of redemption is worked out on God's side. Since Christ is solid with God, what He achieves and suffers has the whole guarantee of God behind it. He is God invading a rebel world and restoring the rebel creature to fellowship with Himself. But the solidarity of Christ as Man with ourselves is no less of the essence of redemption. Professor Hodges is clearly right in seeing the pattern of Atonement as closely related to our union with our Lord, although there may sometimes be grounds for suspecting that he is so anxious to assert the fact of 'Christ in us,' that he may have done less than justice to the complementary truth of 'Christ for us.' And some theologians will feel the need to assert more strongly than others (or is it simply a case of assertion in a different idiom or in a different way?) that our solidarity with Christ in no sense weakens the two sides of the division between Creator and creature.

At this point it might appear as if all has been said, but we must still inquire what is involved in our response to the Divine initiative. It may well be asked whether there is a human response which is not evoked by God's action in Christ, and whether, if this be the case, it can be described as our response at all. Evangelical systems of theology, classically sensitive to the idea of 'merit' in any form, have always been on their guard against any interpretation of faith as a 'work,' however special it may be in kind or in degree.[1]

The status of the human response to the Divine initiative is the decisive question which divides the two traditional theologies of grace, known as Monergism and Synergism respectively.[2] The former stresses the Divine initiative as the sole significant factor in the situation, while the latter insists upon the need for man's co-operation. St. Paul states both sides in the form of a paradox: 'Work out your own salvation in fear and trembling, for it is God that worketh in you to will and to do of His good pleasure.'[3] There is a response which man must make, faith, acceptance, surrender, committal, or whatever name we may assign to it; but in the last resort this is no unprompted or unmotivated act. It is a response to the drawing-power of Christ; and in a sense God is involved in the act of response as well as in the initiative which evokes it, and which remains wholly and solely His.

If systematic theology, ancient or modern, has done nothing to remove the element of paradox here, there are certainly considerations which will serve to make it less opaque or less intractable. The first is drawn from philosophy, though I suspect that the suggestion which follows might not necessarily commend itself to all philosophers. What do we mean when we speak of an act as our own? Clearly we do not mean an unmotivated act. Whether or not such 'capricious freedom'

[1] See the admirable discussion of the problem in G. Aulén, *The Faith of the Christian Church*, pp. 318–22.

[2] See N. P. Williams, *The Grace of God*. The terms themselves appear to date from the classical period of Lutheranism.

[3] Phil. ii. 12–13.

F

(as Sidgwick called it) really exists, we should not normally assign to actions of this kind any specially high valuation.[1] Included in an act which we should nevertheless describe as our own are factors dependent upon heredity and environment; in fact, our whole life-situation (*Sitz im Leben*). Just because we are creatures, we cannot, as it were, jump out of our skins, and for the same reason, the freedom which we possess is a conditioned freedom. Yet, without 'us,' 'our actions' could not come into existence at all, and we can align ourselves with certain elements in our heredity and environment and not with others. The care and education of children is largely concerned with the attempt to help them to accept some and to reject other elements in their environment. Within the complex of influences with which we are confronted is what God has done for our redemption. If, then, our act of response is motivated by God's initiative, it may reasonably be maintained that it does not thereby cease to be our response.

If our argument in the preceding chapters has been in any way sound, the Divine initiative will be seen to be a good deal more than any factor involved in human motivation, though this may not deprive the parallel of its value. The problem then becomes one of determining whether there is any 'collision' between God's initiative and man's response. By 'collision' in this sense is meant the kind of situation which arises when one billiard ball strikes another or in the old puzzle of

[1] See the article on 'The Freedom of the Will' by D. M. Baillie reprinted from the *Scottish Journal of Theology*, Vol. 4 in *The Theology of the Sacraments and Other Papers*, pp. 132-3.

what happens when an irresistible force meets an immovable mass. If, however, both factors in the situation are conceived in personal terms, then the difficulty can be met to some considerable extent. Collision in the exceptionable sense only arises in the impingement of impersonal forces or the contact between a person and a thing such as tripping over a carpet or colliding with a car door, or between human beings when one or the other is treated at less than a personal level—as a hand, a pen, or a tool. Any deep and significant personal relationship involves elements both of Monergism and Syngerism without any taint of collision in the sense noted above. A successful pupil may say to his tutor in gratitude, 'I could not have done it without you.' That is a statement with Monergistic implications; and it may well be true that without the stimulus and inspiration of his tutor the student might well have remained (academically speaking) an unguided missile. But the tutor (if he is wise as well as learned) might well reply, 'Nonsense, my dear fellow, you did it yourself'; and that would be true too, for it is an undeniable fact that the student did the work and wrote the papers. The implications of such a statement are at best Synergistic. There may be paradox here, but there is not contradiction. It is a faint parallel in the sphere of personal relationships to what Donald Baillie called 'the Paradox of Grace.'[1] Both explanations ring true, but both describe the same situation from a different point of view. The Monergist views the whole process of being redeemed 'end-on' or 'from above below,' and in so doing sees more deeply

[1] D. M. Baillie, *God was in Christ*, pp. 114–18.

into its implications. On the other hand, the Synergist views the whole process as it were in cross-section, and may well have a truer insight into the basic ingredients of the total situation. The Christian understanding of grace has historically oscillated between these two poles. The Pauline paradox may be interpreted as a kind of stereoscopic picture of the two aspects of the doctrine.

It remains to discuss the doctrine of Justification by Faith alone. Inevitably some aspects of the subject must be omitted and I propose (unpardonably as some may think) to omit almost entirely the important question of its application to the doctrines of the Church and Sacraments. The term itself is not found in Scripture, though its champions would claim with good reason that it is as much in harmony with Scripture as the famous *homoousion* of the Nicene Creed. Discussion on the subject has recently arisen within the Church of England after a period in which the Reformation disputes appeared to be largely a matter of terms.[1] There is a splendidly irenic treatment by Professor Hodges in his fine book, *The Pattern of Atonement*.[2]

There is little doubt that misunderstandings over terminology have done something to sharpen the issue. As Sanday and Headlam long ago pointed out, the lexicography of the verb *dikaioun* in Septuagintal and New Testament Greek establishes decisively the meaning 'to acquit' or 'to deem righteous.'[3] On the other

[1] See *The Doctrine of Justification by Faith* (edited by W. M. F. Scott), especially the essay by F. J. Taylor, to which I am particularly indebted.   [2] H. A. Hodges, op. cit., pp. 60–82.
[3] Sanday and Headlam, *Romans* (I.C.C.), pp. 28–31.

hand, its Latin equivalent, *justificare*, seemed to point equally decisively to the translation 'to make righteous.' Yet Biblical usage is not necessarily bound down to matters of lexicography, and authorities as different as Professors Hodges and Snaith (the latter on the basis of a careful study of Hebrew vocabulary and usage) incline to the view that the term might be extended to cover a greater range of the saving activity of God in Christ.[1] But the problem of terminology was at least a complicating factor both for the Reformers and the Council of Trent. Neither wished to dispute, or to fail to account theologically for, the whole of the Christian life. The Council of Trent (and, in general, Roman Catholic expositions of the theology of St. Paul) treated justification as a kind of portmanteau term to cover the totality of the Christian life, whereas for the Reformers it was in varying degrees distinguished from sanctification.[2]

While it is possible that in some passages the thought of St. Paul to some extent outran his vocabulary, it is clear that in the main his use of the word is concerned primarily with the question of the new status. It answers the question, 'How can I, a lost and guilty sinner, come before a just and holy God?' with the reply, 'I am justified freely by faith alone through the merits of Christ.' The antithesis to justification by faith is what Dom Gregory Dix once somewhat irreverently described as 'justification by dodges.'[3] In

[1] H. A. Hodges, op. cit., pp. 62–4; N. H. Snaith, *The Distinctive Ideas of the Old Testament*, pp. 161–73.

[2] See F. Prat, S.J., *The Theology of St. Paul.*

[3] G. Dix, *The Shape of the Liturgy*, p. 625, n. 1.

that case, perhaps the principle, so hotly debated at the Reformation, might be described as a theological truism. But is this all that is really involved?

Perhaps I may be forgiven for introducing a closer study of the subject by a personal reminiscence. At the Anglo-Scandinavian Conference held near Helsinki in 1952, I remember describing the teaching on justification by faith which I had received at Wycliffe Hall as a 'theology of the threshold,' and was not a little surprised at the time to find this view described as 'too subjective, too pietistic.' Another member of the conference offered an interpretation of the doctrine which I recognized (correctly, as it happened) as a summary of the famous essay of Father George Congreve, S.S.J.E., on 'The Christian Life considered as a Response.' This was heartily welcomed by the Lutherans present as exactly conveying their meaning. To have the teaching of Wycliffe Hall passed over in favour of an interpretation of the doctrine by a Cowley Father was indeed surprising and represented a challenge to rethink the doctrine which I could not well ignore.

There might at first sight be much to support the opinion rejected by the Lutherans. The Evangelical tradition in the Church of England in which I was brought up was certainly (like Lutheranism itself at some periods) much under the influence of Pietism both in theology and experience. There is the experience of Luther himself, of the Wesleys, and of countless other souls, so sympathetically delineated by Professor Hodges, who found themselves in border-line situations and were driven to ask threshold questions. The contrast between the once-born and twice-born types of religious experience, which originally derives from F. W. Newman, has been copiously illustrated from the psychological point of view by William James, although he makes little serious attempt to come to grips with the specifically theological implications of his theme.[1] Justification and conversion are certainly related themes, although Professor Hodges would not lack sound Evangelical support for his distinction between the fact and the consciousness of justification. Theologically, too, the 'peak approach' to the Cross has naturally been associated with a 'crisis' interpretation of the Christian life, whereas a 'tableland' view of the Atonement which links together the total pattern of the Incarnate life of Christ fits more easily into an interpretation of the Christian life in terms of progress.

A reasonably strong case might therefore be made out for the interpretation of justification rejected by my Lutheran friends. Further reflexion, however, suggests that it represents at best only part of the truth. It would be a bold over-simplification to suggest that the issue between the Reformers and the Council of Trent, or, to put the matter more widely, between Evangelical and Catholic, is confined to the distinction between once-born and twice-born, or different valuations of conversion and its implications. Yet, on the other hand, what is involved is more than two ways of expressing an identical truth, widened by conflicting

[1] William James, *Varieties of Religious Experience*. The distinction appears to derive from F. W. Newman, *The Soul: its Sorrows and Aspirations*. See, however, the brief but trenchant criticisms of its value in Bishop Stephen Neill, *The Unfinished Task*, pp. 40–1.

terminologies and embittered, as far as the Reformation was concerned, by ecclesiastical, political, and ecclesiological differences. It is rather two different approaches to the whole texture of the Christian life, two divergent patterns of Christian spirituality.

This divergence of pattern may be illustrated in a number of ways. The first concerns the relation of being and doing. The Catholic seems to approach being through doing, and urges that there can be no open road to being except through doing. 'Sow an action, reap a habit; sow a habit, reap a character; sow a character, reap a destiny' appears to be a mere ethical commonplace. On the other hand, the Evangelical has classically insisted that, apart from right being, right doing is cut off at the roots. He would therefore maintain (consistently with his premises) that a radical restoration in the realm of being was the necessary presupposition of right conduct. Right action flows from right being; right being is not, as it were, merely built up out of right actions. This difference of starting-point has been sharpened by charge and counter-charge, often based upon the most grotesque misunderstandings. The Catholic will be accused of will-worship (whatever that may mean) or of enthroning the idea of merit; the Evangelical of antinomian tendencies. It may even be, as Professor Hodges has suggested, that there is a difference between the two methodologies on the respective positions assigned to goodness and holiness. The Catholic thinks primarily of goodness as a limited objective which (under God) is within his reach, and dares to hope that some measure of holiness may possibly emerge. The Evangelical takes with the utmost possible seriousness the New Testament description of Christians as 'called to be saints,' and dares to believe that, receiving the greater from God, the lesser will be added unto him. Does this perhaps throw some light upon the otherwise terrible Anglican article on works before justification? Certainly the distinction does not lack its bearing upon the relation between justification and sanctification.

A similar divergence of outlook can be expressed in terms of a contrast between incorporation and appropriation. No Evangelical would wish to deny the validity and significance either of the Pauline technical term 'in Christ,' or of the image of the Body and its members. That would argue a high degree of 'unscripturalness' on the part of those who seek above all to be faithful to the Bible. But he is usually much on his guard against any attempt to over-press or over-expound either phrase.[1] Here his difficulty is a twofold one. He would claim that even in the realm of redemption the difference between God and man, or between the Creator and the creature, remains and must be respected. He is not in the least concerned to deny the closeness of our reconciled relationship in Christ, but he becomes uneasy when the implications of the Pauline image of the Body are pressed too far. Ontological incorporation or any similar over-application of the metaphor seems to him either to blur the distinctness

[1] The most recent detailed study of New Testament usage from an Evangelical point of view (Irish Presbyterian) is to be found in Ernest Best, *One Body in Christ*. Criticism of some theological inferences from the Pauline images may be found in D. M. Baillie, *The Theology of the Sacraments*, pp. 61–6, and L. Newbigin, *The Reunion of the Church*, pp. 55–83.

G

between God and man (as in the use of the language of deification, traditional though this may be) or to reduce the relationship which we enjoy in and with Christ even by implication below the level of the personal. Thus, side by side with (and even in preference to) incorporation, he is anxious to assert the complementary truth of appropriation interpreted as an operation which only exists between persons. If the image of the Body and its members expresses superbly the closeness of the bond which unites the Redeemer and the redeemed, he refuses to take it in isolation from the corresponding metaphor of the Head and the members lest it should lead to a loss of understanding of the highest levels at which our redemption becomes operative. It cannot be too strongly emphasized that so far as St. Paul is concerned, the personal encounter on the Damascus road is never far from his mind. If it cannot be seriously maintained either that an Evangelical would wish to deny anything that could colourably be maintained under the head of incorporation, or that a Catholic would be chary of accepting anything which is rightly included under appropriation, the distinction nevertheless describes a major difference of starting-point which recurs at many and often unsuspected points in their respective approaches to Christian spirituality. Would it be too misleading to express the difference somewhat as follows? The Evangelical approaches incorporation through appropriation, whereas the Catholic instinctively reverses the order.

A further difference seems to arise with respect to the methodology of the life of grace. It is not seriously in dispute that the Christian life includes sanctification. But differences arise in the method of approach to the subject. The Catholic finds no difficulty in speaking of impartation. The righteousness of Christ is made available to us in such a way as to become, as it were, ontologically our own. Such infused grace is a direct corollary of our incorporation into Christ. This appears to him a plain and straightforward account of the matter. The Evangelical, however, prefers the New Testament term, imputation, and is inclined to suspect over-simplification or, what is worse, the confusion of two distinct realities in the Catholic account of the matter.

I have sometimes wondered whether this divergence of attitude may not be illustrated by two different attitudes to gifts. I inherit a piece of furniture. I may argue, 'It was Aunt Jane's, but now it is mine,' and therefore treat it as in all respects as one of my own possessions. Or I can say, 'It is mine, but it was Aunt Jane's,' and therefore hold it somewhat apart in my mind from articles which I have bought for myself. The illustration is, of course, trivial, but it may serve to illustrate two quite distinct attitudes in such matters. It may perhaps have a bearing upon the infinitely greater question of the distinction between impartation and imputation. Both sides agree that the righteousness of Christ is in some real way made available to us. The language of imputation insists that although it is made available to us, it still remains the righteousness of Christ; it is, in effect, righteousness 'on lease-lend,' whereas the language of impartation claims that although, of course, Christ is its source and origin, it is also in a sense *our* righteousness. Once again the two types of Christian spirituality can be misrepresented. The standard charge of reintroducing merit or works will be raised against the Catholic, whereas the Evangelical will be accused of teaching a righteousness which is fictional or even unreal.

The difference may be further illustrated by two points upon which Luther laid some considerable stress, although it may be fair to point out that an Anglican Evangelical would probably not feel himself committed to every statement of the great continental Reformer. Luther always insisted that man was *in via* and not yet *in gloria*, and drew a careful distinction between the theology of the Cross and the theology of glory. The Christian life here below must always be seen under the form of the Cross, and therefore Christian theology always issues in paradox. Here at least Kierkegaard was not untrue to his Lutheran heritage. From this point of view the whole attempt of Catholic theology to provide an ontology of grace is considered to be an illicit anticipation of the theology of glory. Christian existence under the Cross cannot be explained ontologically; it is through-and-through eschatological. Some of the exchanges of view at the Lund Conference which approximated most nearly to a meeting of minds were concerned with the application of this distinction to the doctrine of the Church.

This eschatological interpretation of the Christian life appears to many minds to be a natural corollary of a similar understanding of the Cross. God has won the decisive victory in Christ and yet 'we see not all things put under His feet.' We are living in the period between D-day and V-day, in the overlap of the ages, and are therefore (in Luther's sense) still *in via*. Evangelicals would therefore regard the idea of imputation as a truer reflexion of this aspect of Christian existence than the concept of impartation, which might well appear to harmonize more readily with the theology of glory.

A second line of approach to justification by faith is illustrated by Luther's description of redeemed man as *simul justus et peccator* (both righteous and a sinner). Here we may return to the Lutheran objection to the notion of justification by faith as a 'theology of the threshold.' Luther's description cannot be replaced by the phrase *quondam peccator, nunc justus* ('once a sinner, now righteous') without travesty. For the threshold-situation turns out to be a standing condition of the spiritual life. For Luther man is both, permanently and inescapably both, just because he is still *in via*. The eschatology of the Cross with its double aspect, the victory which is intensively decisive, but extensively incomplete, involved for him a similar eschatology of the Christian life 'both righteous and a sinner.' Each issues in a paradox which finds its resolution only in life under the Cross. On the other hand, consistently with his own premises, the Catholic will maintain that the more a man is the one, the less he will be the other. The eschatological paradox is smoothed out in terms of an ontology of grace; the double polarity of the Christian life, its 'is' and 'is not' is interpreted as a process from less to more.

The scope of this book has inevitably meant that the preceding discussion has been unduly compressed and the concepts and terms employed may be unfamiliar to many readers. It will, however, be found upon reflexion to shed light upon many points of Christian life and thought upon which profound differences seem to arise. It may possibly prove of some help in interpreting to each other two main types of Christian spirituality which the Church of England unites within itself.

But justification is 'by faith alone' (*sola fide*), and the articles as well as the homily to which they refer align the Church of England with the formula which Luther described as the point on which the Church stands or falls (*articulus stantis aut cadentis ecclesiae*). The problem here lies in the extent to which the adjective 'alone' can legitimately be pressed. It is clearly polemical, and represents a counterblast to any doctrine of justification by merits or by works, or any mediating view which sets faith and works on an equality as parallel principles of justification. It has, however, been taken by its critics in much wider and more questionable senses. It can, for example, scarcely be maintained that the *sola fide* of Luther and the *sola gratia* of Calvin are at loggerheads with each other. It is not concerned to deny either the Divine provision or the Divine initiative. While it certainly excludes, in practice as well as in theology, what Professor Hodges has described as 'salvation by sacraments,' it would be untrue to allege that it leads theologically to the under-valuation of sacraments, and still less that it ought logically to lead to their complete abandonment. The notion that the only consistent Evangelicals are the Salvation Army or the Society of Friends completely misconceives the application of the principle to sacramental theology. It should hardly need to be added that the doctrine of justification by faith alone is not identical with the sub-Christian idea of salvation without works. What is at stake here is not the necessity for good works, but their place in relation to faith as the instrument of our justification. Here faith is prior to good works in the economy of salvation. They are regarded as the consequents and not as the antecedents or even as the collaterals of faith in our justification.

So far as the content of faith is concerned, there is certainly a difference of emphasis between Catholic and Evangelical, though it is probable that there is more common ground between them than has sometimes been imagined.[1]

The Catholic conception of faith lays considerable emphasis upon its intellectual consent. Thomist theology defines faith as 'thinking with assent' (*cum assensione cogitare*). An important distinction is drawn between 'explicit faith,' considered as the detailed affirmation of a whole body of belief, and 'implicit faith,' which combines a general acceptance of what the Church teaches together with a more rudimentary grasp of its principal heads. But, as Professor Hodges rightly observes, it is difficult to regard faith in this sense as much more than the *sine qua non* of justification. 'He that cometh to God must believe that He is, and that He is the rewarder of them that seek after Him.'[2] The distinction (familiar in Evangelical circles) between

---

[1] On faith see the discussions by H. A. Hodges, op. cit., pp. 83–101; F. J. Taylor, op. cit., pp. 21–4; G. Aulén, op. cit., pp. 22–30 and 73–9.　　　[2] Heb. xi. 6.

belief about God and belief in God or, slightly more technically, between the 'faith which is believed' (*fides quae creditur*) and 'the faith by which it is believed' (*fides qua creditur*) makes what is fundamentally the same point. Yet no Christian will hesitate to use the phrase' 'the Christian faith' to describe Christianity as a coherent system of belief, and the element of assent is not lacking from the description of faith given in such a book as Bishop Aulén's *Faith of the Christian Church*.

On the other hand, the Evangelical doctrine of faith assigns to 'confidence' the role occupied by 'assent' in the Catholic tradition. This starting-point at least approximates more closely to the spiritual realities of the Christian life. It lifts the idea of faith beyond the region of a mere *sine qua non*. It has, however, given rise to considerable misunderstanding for which some justification may be found in Pietism and in certain other movements in theology such as Ritschlianism, which arose from the impact of the enlightenment upon the Evangelical tradition. A recent description of the Lutheran conception of faith as a 'sentiment of confidence without rational preamble or practical fruit'[1] borders on the grotesque. It would be difficult to reconcile the phrase 'without rational preamble' with the massive systems of Christian doctrine based upon the principle of justification by faith alone from Reformation times onwards. The charge could only be substantiated if the element of assent were completely lacking in the Evangelical tradition. Nor would it be

[1] A. II. Rees, *Theology Occasional Papers* (*New Series*), No. 2, criticized by E. G. Rupp, *Studies in the Making of the English Protestant Tradition*, pp. 171–94.

any easier to defend the second half of this criticism. Luther himself waged unceasing war against the Antinomians as well as other left-wing groups of the continental Reformation. If for him the Law is not part of the Gospel, it is nevertheless part of the Christian revelation. The Formula of Concord, the document which gathers together the fruits of the formative period of Lutheranism, speaks of a third use of the Law 'for the regenerate.' Quite apart from the Lutheran Reformation, the Evangelical tradition certainly contains a theology and practice of sanctification, although both in its general pattern and typical forms of expression, it may differ widely from its Catholic counterpart.

Professor Hodges also comments upon this interpretation of faith (*fides*) as confidence (*fiducia*) and supports his criticisms by quotations from classical documents of the Reformation. He claims that 'these unfortunate Protestant definitions' are 'unsuccessful attempts to formulate a truth' rather than 'successful attempts to formulate a heresy.' Here I think it possible that he has missed the crucial point. The passage from Calvin from which he starts certainly defines faith as 'a firm and sure knowledge of God's good will towards us,' but adds the careful qualifications 'founded upon the free promises given in Jesus Christ, and revealed to our minds and sealed in our hearts by the Holy Ghost.' To Calvin, therefore, faith is a founded confidence, 'revealed . . . and sealed in our hearts by the Holy Ghost.' The confidence of which he speaks is certainly no mere human quality. The Godward reference of faith seems to be fully safeguarded by this definition. While the language of the Anglican homily to which

he next turns seems less carefully guarded, it still makes
the Godward reference of faith quite explicit. 'He hath
accepted us again into His favour . . . not for our own
merits and deserts, but only and solely for the merits
of Christ's death and Passion.' Faith is 'a sure trust
and confidence in the mercies of God.' Even in contexts in which faith is primarily interpreted in terms of
confidence or trust, justification by faith cannot be
understood apart from its reference to the merits of
Christ. Justification, faith, and the merits of Christ
(*propter Christum*, or 'for Christ's sake') belong in-
separably together. Thus the Evangelical definitions
quoted by Professor Hodges, seen in the theological
context which they themselves provide, do not prove
to be as unfortunate as he seems to find them. The
interpretation of faith in terms of confidence or trust
forms part of the Reformation return to a richer and
more Pauline conception of faith. Here is confidence,
but it is no merely subjective or human feeling; it is
a founded confidence which rests upon the objective
action of God in Christ, and it is realized within us by
the operation of the Holy Spirit.

A third strand in the meaning of faith is 'self-com-
mittal' or 'self-surrender.' Under this head Professor
Hodges discusses the example of Abraham, which
serves as the *locus classicus* of faith in the New Testament. Bishop Aulén also includes 'a turning and
commitment to God' in the concept of justifying faith,
though he admits that its place in Evangelical theology
has often been obscured by the fear of converting faith
itself into a human work. This is probably more true
of Lutheran than of Anglican theology. Pietism has

certainly borne consistent witness to this aspect of faith. The experience itself is obviously basic to all types of Christian spirituality; the distinctive feature of Evangelical theology is its inclusion under the rubric of justifying faith.

Thus the Evangelical emphasis upon 'faith alone' turns out, upon closer inspection, to be considerably richer than might at first sight appear. The restrictive adjective is simply a polemical side-glance at different conceptions of the instrument of justification, and has been interpreted by its critics more narrowly than its champions ever intended. Such a use of theological italics might well seem dangerous or even misleading, but the Reformers at least believed that they had good reason for their use, and might legitimately expect that the phrase would not be taken out of its proper context. Yet side by side with this negative restriction went, as we have seen, a notable enrichment of the positive content of faith as a result of the recovery of the Pauline perspective.

Thomism and some mediating views, however, move in a different direction. We have seen that the emphasis upon the aspect of faith as assent seems to confine it to the rational preamble of the Christian faith and is more appropriately described as the *sine qua non* of justification than as justification itself. Some enrichment of the idea is obviously called for, particularly as the content of Justification is extended a good deal more widely in Catholic circles than is customary in Evangelical theology. St. Thomas himself supplemented the concept of faith as assent by the idea of 'faith informed by love' (*fides formata caritate*). There is at first sight good Pauline precedent for this particular expansion. The Apostle certainly speaks of 'faith working through love' and groups together faith, hope, and love in his hymn to heavenly love.[1] As the three theological virtues, the Pauline triad exercised a considerable influence upon theology. It is obvious that love must occupy the centre of the stage in any full account of the Christian life. Yet, whatever the merits of this formulation, it has been consistently rejected by Evangelical theologians as a definition of *justifying* faith. In this tradition, as we have seen, the limits of justification are set less widely than in Roman Catholic theology. Faith and love do not, as it were, form two halves of a single whole in such a way that the content of the one can be filled out by reference to the other. Faith is regarded as primary, and love, like the other Christian virtues, springs from it as flower from root. It might indeed be objected that St. Paul enthrones love rather than faith, but further reflexion suggests that the Pauline lyric and the Evangelical doctrine of justifying faith are concerned with different questions. Evangelical theology is related to the logic of the spiritual life as it is lived *in via*, and therefore stresses the dependence of love upon faith, whereas in this passage St. Paul, while not neglecting its relevance to the day-to-day life of the Church at Corinth, looks ahead to life *in gloria* when we shall know as we are known. In that consummation faith obviously yields pride of place to love. Questions of spiritual priority *in via* and of ultimate significance *in gloria* may require different answers.

A similar confusion between antecedent and conse-

[1] Gal. v. 6; 1 Cor. xiii.

quent, or more exactly, the juxtaposition of two qualities, one of which really depends upon the other, may be found in Jeremy Taylor's sermon, '*Fides Formata;* or Faith working by Love.' His theme is that 'justifying faith contains in itself obedience.' In the light of the clear-cut distinction between justification as the ground and sanctification as the fruit of the Christian life, Evangelical theology would probably feel bound to reject all such attempts to fill out the picture. While a full account of the Christian life would certainly include love, obedience, and the rest of the Christian virtues, their place would rather lie at a later stage of theological inquiry. Attempts to bracket faith with any other quality in the matter of justification would only serve (on Evangelical premises) to cloud the issue with which the formula 'justification by faith alone' is concerned. The choice here seems to lie between a wider conception of faith framed on New Testament lines, and a more restricted meaning filled out by the addition of other Christian virtues.

Such, then, are the principal questions involved in the application of the Atonement, so far as they bear directly upon the discussion of the meaning of the Cross contained in the preceding chapters. Fuller treatment would certainly have involved a consideration of the doctrines of the Church and the Sacraments where again interesting conclusions seem to emerge. A certain cohesion between the two parts of our subject can be discerned. The eschatological understanding of the Cross seems to correspond to a similar eschatology of the Christian life. God's initiative in redeeming action evokes man's response of faith, a committal involving assent and ripening into confidence, from which flows the actuality of a renewed life. Here we have been increasingly concerned with the question of the whole texture of the Christian life. The existence of permanent differences of approach on this matter seems undeniable, and any neat and tidy synthesis in the field of Christian spirituality may well prove undeniable while we remain *in via*. Yet the realities with which we are concerned are one and indivisible, even where our interpretations must remain unreconciled. The experience of being redeemed in Christ unites, even if our theologies of redemption are at many points divergent. Each must seek to interpret what he sees in the best possible idiom and terminology, but prior to what he sees and seeks to interpret is what God has wrought in us all. Our differences arise from the fact that we are still *in via*, and can therefore only see partially. They will find their resolution when God brings us into glory, for then we shall see face to face and know even as we are known.